ISBN 978-1-331-03695-1
PIBN 10136606

1 MONTH OF FREE READING

at

www.ForgottenBooks.com

By purchasing this book you are eligible for one month membership to ForgottenBooks.com, giving you unlimited access to our entire collection of over 700,000 titles via our web site and mobile apps.

To claim your free month visit:

www.forgottenbooks.com/free136606

Similar Books Are Available from
www.forgottenbooks.com

Poems
by Edgar Allan Poe

The Complete Poetical Works and Letters of John Keats
by John Keats

Erotica
by Arthur Clark Kennedy

The Complete Poetical Works of John Milton
by John Milton

One Hundred Poems of Kabir
by Kabir

The Barons' Wars, Nymphidia, and Other Poems
by Michael Drayton

A Book of English Poetry
by George Beaumont

Poems: Sonnets, Lyrics, and Miscellaneous
by Edward Blackadder

The Book of Fairy Poetry
by Dora Owen

Chinese Poems
by Charles Budd

Coleridge's The Rime of the Ancient Mariner
And Other Poems, by Samuel Taylor Coleridge

Complaints; Containing Sundrie Small Poemes of the Worlds Vanitie
Whereof the Next Page Maketh Mention, by Edmund Spenser

The Complete Poetical Works of Geoffrey Chaucer
Now First Put Into Modern English, by John S. P. Tatlock

Cursor Mundi (The Cursor of the World)
A Northumbrian Poem of the XIVth Century, by Richard Morris

The Defence of the Bride Other Poems
by Anna Katharine Green

The Divine Comedy, Vol. 1
by Dante Alighieri

The Duke of Gandia
by Algernon Charles Swinburne

Eanthe
A Tale of the Druids, and Other Poems, by Sandford Earle

The Earthly Paradise
A Poem, by William Morris

The English Poems of George Herbert
Newly Arranged in Relation to His Life, by George Herbert Palmer

SELECTED POEMS

SELECTED POEMS

by
JOHN DAVIDSON

1905

JOHN LANE

The Bodley Head

**LONDON &
NEW YORK**

Printed from Plates made in the United
States of America by the Ballantyne Press

CONTENTS

CONTENTS

SELECTED POEMS

A BALLAD OF HELL

' A LETTER from my love to-day!
　　Oh, unexpected, dear appeal!'
She struck a happy tear away,
　　And broke the crimson seal.

' My love, there is no help on earth,
　　No help in heaven; the dead-man's bell
Must toll our wedding; our first hearth
　　Must be the well-paved floor of hell.'

The colour died from out her face,
　　Her eyes like ghostly candles shone;
She cast dread looks about the place,
　　Then clenched her teeth and read right on.

' I may not pass the prison door;
　　Here must I rot from day to day,
Unless I wed whom I abhor,
　　My cousin, Blanche of Valencay.

' At midnight with my dagger keen
　　I'll take my life; it must be so.
Meet me in hell to-night, my queen,
　　For weal and woe.'

A BALLAD OF HELL

She laughed although her face was wan,
  She girded on her golden belt,
She took her jewelled ivory fan,
  And at her glowing missal knelt.

Then rose, 'And am I mad?' she said;
  She broke her fan, her belt untied;
With leather girt herself instead,
  And stuck a dagger at her side.

She waited, shuddering in her room,
  Till sleep had fallen on all the house.
She never flinched; she faced her doom:
  They two must sin to keep their vows.

Then out into the night she went,
  And stooping crept by hedge and tree;
Her rose-bush flung a snare of scent,
  And caught a happy memory.

She fell, and lay a minute's space;
  She tore the sward in her distress;
The dewy grass refreshed her face;
  She rose and ran with lifted dress.

She started like a morn-caught ghost
  Once when the moon came out and stood
To watch; the naked road she crossed,
  And dived into the murmuring wood.

A BALLAD OF HELL

The branches snatched her streaming cloak;
    A live thing shrieked; she made no stay!
She hurried to the trysting-oak—
    Right well she knew the way.

Without a pause she bared her breast,
    And drove her dagger home and fell,
And lay like one that takes her rest,
    And died and wakened up in hell.

She bathed her spirit in the flame,
    And near the centre took her post;
From all sides to her ears there came,
    The dreary anguish of the lost.

The devil started at her side,
    Comely, and tall, and black as jet.
' I am young Malespina's bride;
    Has he come hither yet?'

' My poppet, welcome to your bed.'
    ' Is Malespina here?'
' Not he! To-morrow he must wed
    His cousin Blanche, my dear!'

' You lie, he died with me to-night.'
    ' Not he! it was a plot.' ' You lie.'
' My dear, I never lie outright.'
    ' We died at midnight he and I.'

The devil went.   Without a groan
   She, gathered up in one fierce prayer,
Took root in hell's midst all alone,
   And waited for him there.

She dared to make herself at home
   Amidst the wail, the uneasy stir.
The blood-stained flame that filled the dome,
   Scentless and silent, shrouded her.

How long she stayed I cannot tell;
   But when she felt his perfidy,
She marched across the floor of hell;
   And all the damned stood up to see.

The devil stopped her at the brink:
   She shook him off; she cried, 'Away!'
' My dear, you have gone mad, I think.'
   ' I was betrayed: I will not stay.'

Across the weltering deep she ran;
   A stranger thing was never seen:
The damned stood silent to a man;
   They saw the great gulf set between.

To her it seemed a meadow fair;
   And flowers sprang up about her feet.
She entered heaven; she climbed the stair
   And knelt down at the mercy-seat.

A BALLAD OF HELL

Seraphs and saints with one great voice
 Welcomed that soul that knew not fear;
Amazed to find it could rejoice,
 Hell raised a hoarse half-human cheer.

A BALLAD OF HEAVEN

He wrought at one great work for years;
   The world passed by with lofty look:
Sometimes his eyes were dashed with tears;
   Sometimes his lips with laughter shook.

His wife and child went clothed in rags,
   And in a windy garret starved:
He trod his measures on the flags,
   And high on heaven his music carved.

Wistful he grew but never feared;
   For always on the midnight skies
His rich orchestral score appeared
   In stars and zones and galaxies.

He thought to copy down his score·
   The moonlight was his lamp: he said,
‘ Listen, my love;’ but on the floor
   His wife and child were lying dead.

Her hollow eyes were open wide;
   He deemed she heard with special zest:
Her death’s-head infant coldly eyed
   The desert of her shrunken breast.

' Listen, my love: my work is done;
    I tremble as I touch the page
To sign the sentence of the sun
    And crown the great eternal age.

' The slow adagio begins;
    The winding-sheets are ravelled out
That swathe the minds of men, the sins
    That wrap their rotting souls about.

' The dead are heralded along;
    With silver trumps and golden drums,
And flutes and oboes, keen and strong,
    My brave andante singing comes.

' Then like a python's sumptuous dress
    The frame of things is cast away,
And out of Time's obscure distress,
    The thundering scherzo crashes Day.

' For three great orchestras I hope
    My mighty music shall be scored:
On three high hills they shall have scope
    With heaven's vault for a sounding-board.

' Sleep well, love; let your eyelids fall;
    Cover the child; goodnight, and if . . .
What?   Speak . . . the traitorous end of all!
    Both . . . cold and hungry . . . cold and stiff!

' But no, God means us well, I trust:
      Dear ones, be happy, hope is nigh:
We are too young to fall to dust,
      And too unsatisfied to die.'

He lifted up against his breast
      The woman's body stark and wan;
And to her withered bosom pressed
      The little skin-clad skeleton.

' You see you are alive,' he cried.
      He rocked them gently to and fro.
' No, no, my love, you have not died;
      Nor you, my little fellow; no.'

Long in his arms he strained his dead
      And crooned an antique lullaby;
Then laid them on the lowly bed,
      And broke down with a doleful cry.

' The love, the hope, the blood, the brain,
      Of her and me, the budding life,
And my great music—all in vain!
      My unscored work, my child, my wife!

' We drop into oblivion,
      And nourish some suburban sod:
My work, this woman, this my son,
      Are now no more: there is no God.

‘ The world's a dustbin; we are due,
  And death's cart waits: be life accurst!’
He stumbled down beside the two,
  And clasping them, his great heart burst.

Straightway he stood at heaven's gate,
  Abashed and trembling for his sin:
I trow he had not long to wait,
  For God came out and led him in.

And then there ran a radiant pair,
  Ruddy with haste and eager-eyed
To meet him first upon the stair—
  His wife and child beatified.

They clad him in a robe of light,
  And gave him heavenly food to eat;
Great seraphs praised him to the height,
  Archangels sat about his feet.

God, smiling, took him by the hand,
  And led him to the brink of heaven:
He saw where systems whirling stand,
  Where galaxies like snow are driven.

Dead silence reigned; a shudder ran
  Through space; Time furled his wearied wings;
A slow adagio then began
  Sweetly resolving troubled things.

The dead were heralded along:
　As if with drums and trumps of flame,
And flutes and oboes keen and strong,
　A brave andante singing came.

Then like a python's sumptuous dress
　The frame of things was cast away,
And out of Time's obscure distress
　The conquering scherzo thundeied Day.

He doubted; but God said 'Even so;
　Nothing is lost that's wrought with tears:
The music that you made below
　Is now the music of the spheres.'

A BALLAD OF A NUN

FROM Eastertide to Eastertide
    For ten long years her patient knees
Engraved the stones—the fittest bride
    Of Christ in all the diocese.

She conquered every earthly lust;
    The abbess loved her more and more;
And, as a mark of perfect trust,
    Made her the keeper of the door.

High on a hill the convent hung,
    Across a duchy looking down,
Where everlasting mountains flung
    Their shadows over tower and town.

The jewels of their lofty snows
    In constellations flashed at night;
Above their crests the moon arose;
    The deep earth shuddered with delight.

Long ere she left her cloudy bed,
    Still dreaming in the orient land,
On many a mountain's happy head
    Dawn lightly laid her rosy hand.

The adventurous sun took Heaven by storm;
   Clouds scattered largesses of rain;
The sounding cities, rich and warm,
   Smouldered and glittered in the plain.

Sometimes it was a wandering wind,
   Sometimes the fragrance of the pine,
Sometimes the thought how others sinned,
   That turned her sweet blood into wine.

Sometimes she heard a serenade
   Complaining sweetly far away·
She said, 'A young man woos a maid';
   And dreamt of love till break of day.

Then would she ply her knotted scourge
   Until she swooned; but evermore
She had the same red sin to purge,
   Poor, passionate keeper of the door!

For still night's starry scroll unfurled,
   And still the day came like a flood:
It was the greatness of the world
   That made her long to use her blood.

In winter-time when Lent drew nigh,
   And hill and plain were wrapped in snow,
She watched beneath the frosty sky
   The nearest city nightly glow.

Like peals of airy bells outworn
    Faint laughter died above her head
In gusts of broken music borne:
    ' They keep the Carnival,' she said.

Her hungry heart devoured the town:
    ' Heaven save me by a miracle!
Unless God sends an angel down,
    Thither I go though it were Hell.'

She dug her nails deep in her breast,
    Sobbed, shrieked, and straight withdrew the bar:
A fledgling flying from the nest,
    A pale moth rushing to a star.

Fillet and veil in strips she tore·
    Her golden tresses floated wide;
The ring and bracelet that she wore
    As Christ's betrothed, she cast aside.

' Life's dearest meaning I shall probe;
    Lo! I shall taste of love at last!
Away!' She doffed her outer robe,
    And sent it sailing down the blast.

Her body seemed to warm the wind;
    With bleeding feet o'er ice she ran:
' I leave the righteous God behind;
    I go to worship sinful man.'

She reached the sounding city's gate;
　　No question did the warder ask:
He passed her in: 'Welcome, wild mate!'
　　He thought her some fantastic mask.

Half-naked through the town she went;
　　Each footstep left a bloody mark;
Crowds followed her with looks intent;
　　Her bright eyes made the torches dark.

Alone and watching in the street
　　There stood a grave youth nobly dressed;
To him she knelt and kissed his feet;
　　Her face her great desire confessed.

Straight to his house the nun he led:
　　'Strange lady, what would you with me?'
'Your love, your love, sweet lord,' she said;
　　'I bring you my virginity.'

He healed her bosom with a kiss;
　　She gave him all her passion's hoard;
And sobbed and murmured ever, 'This
　　Is life's great meaning, dear, my lord.

'I care not for my broken vow;
　　Though God should come in thunder soon,
I am sister to the mountains now,
　　And sister to the sun and moon.'

Through all the towns of Belmarie
    She made a progress like a queen.
' She is,' they said, ' whate'er she be,
    The strangest woman ever seen.

' From fairyland she must have come,
    Or else she is a mermaiden.'
Some said she was a ghoul, and some
    A heathen goddess born again.

But soon her fire to ashes burned;
    Her beauty changed to haggardness;
Her golden hair to silver turned;
    The hour came of her last caress.

At midnight from her lonely bed
    She rose, and said, ' I have had my will.'
The old ragged robe she donned, and fled
    Back to the convent on the hill.

Half-naked as she went before,
    She hurried to the city wall,
Unnoticed in the rush and roar
    And splendour of the carnival.

No question did the warder ask:
    Her ragged robe, her shrunken limb,
Her dreadful eyes!　' It is no mask;
    It is a she-wolf, gaunt and grim!'

She ran across the icy plain;
 Her worn blood curdled in the blast;
Each footstep left a crimson stain;
 The white-faced moon looked on aghast.

She said between her chattering jaws,
 ' Deep peace is mine, I cease to strive;
Oh, comfortable convent laws,
 That bury foolish nuns alive!

' A trowel for my passing-bell,
 A little bed within the wall,
A coverlet of stones; how well
 I there shall keep the Carnival!'

Like tired bells chiming in their sleep,
 The wind faint peals of laughter bore;
She stopped her ears and climbed the steep,
 And thundered at the convent door.

It opened straight: she entered in,
 And at the wardress' feet fell prone:
' I come to purge away my sin;
 Bury me, close me up in stone.'

The wardress raised her tenderly;
 She touched her wet and fast-shut eyes:
' Look, sister; sister, look at me;
 Look; can you see through my disguise?'

She looked and saw her own sad face,
  And trembled, wondering, 'Who art thou?'
' God sent me down to fill your place:
  I am the Virgin Mary now.'

And with the word, God's mother shone:
  The wanderer whispered, 'Mary, hail!'
The vision helped her to put on
  Bracelet and fillet, ring and veil.

You are sister to the mountains now,
  And sister to the day and night;
Sister to God.'   And on the brow
  She kissed her thrice, and left her sight.

While dreaming in her cloudy bed,
  Far in the crimson orient land,
On many a mountain's happy head
  Dawn lightly laid her rosy hand.

A BALLAD OF AN ARTIST'S WIFE

' Sweet wife, this heavy-hearted age
    Is nought to us; we two shall look
To Art, and fill a perfect page
    In Life's ill-written doomsday book.'

He wrought in colour; blood and brain
    Gave fire and might; and beauty grew
And flowered with every magic stain
    His passion on the canvas threw.

They shunned the world and worldly ways:
    He laboured with a constant will;
But few would look, and none would praise,
    Because of something lacking still.

After a time her days with sighs
    And tears o'erflowed; for blighting need
Bedimmed the lustre of her eyes,
    And there were little mouths to feed.

' My bride shall ne'er be common-place,
    He thought, and glanced; and glanced again:
At length he looked her in the face;
    And lo, a woman old and plain!

About this time the world's heart failed—
    The lusty heart no fear could rend;
In every land wild voices wailed,
    And prophets prophesied the end.

' To-morrow or to-day,' he thought,
   ' May be Eternity; and I
Have neither felt nor fashioned aught
    That makes me unconcerned to die.

' With care and counting of the cost
    My life a sterile waste has grown,
Wherein my better dreams are lost
    Like chaff in the Sahara sown

' I must escape this living tomb!
    My life shall yet be rich and free,
And on the very stroke of Doom
    My soul at last begin to be.

' Wife, children, duty, household fires
    For victims of the good and true!
For me my infinite desires,
    Freedom and things untried and new!

' I would encounter all the press
    Of thought and feeling life can show,
The sweet embrace, the aching stress
    Of every earthly joy and woe;

' And from the world's impending wreck
    And out of pain and pleasure weave
Beauty undreamt of, to bedeck
    The Festival of Doomsday Eve.'

He fled, and joined a motley throng
    That held carousal day and night;
With love and wit, with dance and song,
    They snatched a last intense delight.

Passion to mould an age's art,
    Enough to keep a century sweet,
Was in an hour consumed; each heart
    Lavished a life in every beat.

Amazing beauty filled the looks
    Of sleepless women; music bore
New wonder on its wings; and books
    Throbbed with a thought unknown before.

The sun began to smoke and flare
    Like a spent lamp about to die;
The dusky moon tarnished the air;
    The planets withered in the sky.

Earth reeled and lurched upon her road;
    Tigers were cowed, and wolves grew tame;
Seas shrank, and rivers backward flowed,
    And mountain-ranges burst in flame.

The artist's wife, a soul devout,
  To all these things gave little heed;
For though the sun was going out,
  There still were little mouths to feed.

And there were also shrouds to stitch,
  And chares to do; with all her might,
To feed her babes, she served the rich
  And kept her useless tears till night.

But by-and-by her sight grew dim;
  Her strength gave way; in desperate mood
She laid her down to die. 'Tell him,'
  She sighed, 'I fed them while I could.'

The children met a wretched fate;
  Self-love was all the vogue and vaunt,
And charity gone out of date;
  Wherefore they pined and died of want.

Aghast he heard the story: 'Dead!
  All dead in hunger and despair!
I courted misery,' he said;
  ' But here is more than I can bear.'

Then, as he wrought, the stress of woe
  Appeared in many a magic stain;
And all adored his work, for lo,
  Tears mingled now with blood and brain!

' Look, look !' they cried; 'this man can weave
    Beauty from anguish that appals;'
And at the feast of Doomsday Eve
    They hung his pictures in their halls,

And gazed; and came again between
    The faltering dances eagerly;
They said, 'The loveliest we have seen,
    The last, of man's work, we shall see!'

Then was there neither death nor birth;
    Time ceased; and through the ether fell
The smoky sun, the leprous earth—
    A cinder and an icicle.

No wrathful vials were unsealed;
    Silent, the first things passed away:
No terror reigned; no trumpet pealed
    The dawn of Everlasting Day.

The bitter draught of sorrow's cup
    Passed with the seasons and the years;
And Wisdom dried for ever up
    The deep, old fountainhead of tears.

Out of the grave and ocean's bed
    The artist saw the people rise·
And all the living and the dead
    Were borne aloft to Paradise.

He came where on a silver throne
    A spirit sat for ever young;
Before her Seraphs worshipped prone,
    And Cherubs silver censers swung.

He asked, 'Who may this martyr be?
    What votaress of saintly rule?'
A Cherub said, 'No martyr; she
    Had one gift; she was beautiful.'

Then came he to another bower
    Where one sat on a golden seat,
Adored by many a heavenly Power
    With golden censers smoking sweet.

'This was some gallant wench who led
    Faint-hearted folk and set them free?'
'Oh, no! a simple maid,' they said,
    'Who spent her life in charity.'

At last he reached a mansion blest
    Where on a diamond throne, endued
With nameless beauty, one possessed
    Ineffable beatitude.

The praises of this matchless soul
    The sons of God proclaimed aloud;
From diamond censers odours stole;
    And Hierarchs before her bowed.

' Who was she ?'   God himself replied:
  ' In misery her lot was cast;
She lived a woman's life, and died
  Working My work until the last.'

It was his wife.   He said, ' I pray
  Thee, Lord, despatch me now to Hell.'
But God said, ' No; here shall you stay,
  And in her peace for ever dwell.'

A BALLAD OF A WORKMAN

ALL day beneath polluted skies
  He laboured in a clanging town;
At night he read with bloodshot eyes
  And fondly dreamt of high renown.

' My time is filched by toil and sleep;
  ' My heart,' he thought, ' is clogged with dust;
My soul that flashed from out the deep,
  A magic blade, begins to rust.

' For me the lamps of heaven shine;
  For me the cunning seasons care;
The old undaunted sea is mine,
  The stable earth, the ample air.

' Yet a dark street—at either end,
  A bed, an anvil—prisons me,
Until my desperate state shall mend,
  And Death, the Saviour, set me free.

' Better a hundred times to die,
  And sink at once into the mould,
Than like a stagnant puddle lie
  With arabesques of scum enscrolled.

‘ I must go forth and view the sphere
    I own.   What can my courage daunt?
Instead of dying daily here,
    The worst is dying once of want.

‘ I drop the dream of high renown;
    I ask but to possess my soul.’
At dawn he left the silent town,
    And quaking toward the forest stole.

He feared that he might want the wit
    To light on Nature’s hidden hearth,
And deemed his rusty soul unfit
    To win the beauty of the earth.

But when he came among the trees,
    So slowly built, so many-ring’d,
His doubting thought could soar at ease
    In colour steep’d, with passion wing’d.

Occult remembrances awoke
    Of outlaws in the good greenwood,
And antique times of woaded folk
    Began to haunt his brain and blood.

No longer hope appeared a crime:
    He sang; his very heart and flesh
Aspired to join the ends of time,
    And forge and mould the world afresh.

' I dare not choose to run in vain;
    I must continue toward the goal.'
The pulse of life beat strong again,
    And in a flash he found his soul.

' The worker never knows defeat,
    Though unvictorious he may die:
The anvil and the grimy street,
    My destined throne and Calvary!'

Back to the town he hastened, bent—
    So swiftly did his passion change—
On selfless plans.   ' I shall invent
    A means to amplify the range

' Of human power: find the soul wings,
    If not the body!   Let me give
Mankind more mastery over things,
    More thought, more joy, more will to live.'

He overtook upon the way
    A tottering ancient travel-worn:
' Lend me your arm, good youth, I pray;
    I scarce shall see another morn.'

Dread thought had carved his pallid face,
    And bowed his form, and blanched his hair;
In every part he bore some trace,
    Or some deep dint of uncouth care.

The workman led him to his room,
    And would have nursed him. ' No,' he said;
' It is my self-appointed doom
    To die upon a borrowed bed;

' But hear and note my slightest word.
    I am a man without a name.
I saw the Bastille fall; I heard
    The giant Mirabeau declaim.

' I saw the stormy dawn look pale
    Across the sea-bound battle-field,
When through the hissing sleet and hail
    The clarions of Cromwell pealed:

' I watched the deep-souled Puritan
    Grow greater with the desperate strife:
The cannon waked; the shouting van
    Charged home; and victory leapt to life.

' At Seville in the Royal square
    I saw Columbus as he passed
Laurelled to greet the Catholic pair
    Who had believed in him at last:

' I saw the Andalusians fill
    Windows, and roofs, and balconies—
A firmament of faces still,
    A galaxy of wondering eyes:

' For he had found the unknown shore,
    And made the world's great dream come true:
I think that men shall never more
    Know anything so strange and new.

' By meteor light when day had set
    I looked across Angora's plain,
And watched the fall of Bajazet,
    The victory of Tamerlane.

' In that old city where the vine
    Dislodged the seaweed, once I saw
The inexorable Florentine:
    He looked my way; I bent with awe

' Before his glance, for this was he
    Who drained the dregs of sorrow's cup
In fierce disdain; it seemed to me
    A spirit passed, my hair stood up.

' Draw nearer: breath and sight begin
    To fail me: nearer, ere I die.—
I saw the brilliant Saladin,
    Who taught the Christians courtesy;

' And Charlemagne, whose dreaded name,
    I first in far Bokhara heard;
Mohammed, with the eyes of flame,
    The lightning-blow, the thunder-word.

' I saw Him nailed upon a tree,
    Whom once beside an inland lake
I had beheld in Galilee
    Speaking as no man ever spake.

' I saw imperial Cæsar fall;
    I saw the star of Macedon;
I saw from Troy's enchanted wall
    The death of Priam's mighty son.

' I heard in streets of Troy at night
    Cassandra prophesying fire. . .
A flamelit face upon my sight
    Flashes: I see the World's Desire!

' My life ebbs fast: nearer!   I sought
    A means to overmaster fate:
Me, the Egyptian Hermes taught
    In old Hermopolis the Great:

' I pierced to Nature's inmost hearth,
    And wrung from her with toil untold
The soul and substance of the earth,
    The Seed of life, the Seed of gold.

' Until the end I meant to stay;
    But thought has here so small a range;
And I am tired of night and day,
    And tired of men who never change

‛ All earthly hope ceased long ago;
    Yet, like a mother young and fond
Whose child is dead, I ache to know
    If there be anything beyond.

‛ Dark—all is darkness! Are you there?
    Give me your hand.—I choose to die.
This holds my secret—should you dare;
    And this, to bury me. . . . Good-bye.’

Amazement held the workman’s soul;
    He took the alchemist’s bequest—
A light purse and a parchment scroll;
    And watched him slowly sink to rest.

And nothing could he dream or think;
    He went like one bereft of sense,
Till passion overbore the brink
    Of all his wistful continence,

When his strange guest was laid in earth
    And he had read the scroll: ‛ Behold,
I can procure from Nature’s hearth
    The Seed of Life, the Seed of Gold!

‛ For ever young! Now, time and tide
    Must wait for me; my life shall vie
With fate and fortune stride for stride
    Until the sun drops from the sky.

' Gold at a touch!   Nations and kings
     Shall come and go at my command;
  I shall control the secret springs
     Of enterprise in every land;

' And hasten on the Perfect Day:
     Great men may break the galling chains;
  Sweet looks light up the toilsome way;
     But I alone shall hold the reins!

' All fragrance, all delightfulness,
     And all the glory, all the power,
  That sound and colour can express,
     Shall be my ever-growing dower.

' And I shall know, and I shall love
     In every age, in every clime
  All beauty. . . . I, enthroned above
     Humanity, the peer of Time!

' Nay—selfish!   I shall give to men
     The Seed of Life, the Seed of Gold;
  Restore the Golden Age again
     At once, and let no soul grow old.

' But gold were then of no avail,
     And death would cease—unhallowed doom!
  The heady wine of life grow stale,
     And earth become a living tomb!

'And youth would end, and truth decline,
  And only pale illusion rule;
For it is death makes love divine,
  Men human, life so sweet and full!'

He burnt the scroll. 'I shall not cheat
  My destiny. Life, death for me!
The anvil and the grimy street,
  My unknown throne and Calvary!

'Only obedience can be great;
  It brings the Golden Age again:
Even to be still, abiding fate,
  Is kingly ministry to men!

'I drop the dream of high renown:
  A nameless private in the strife,
Life, take me; take me, clanging town;
  And death, the eager zest of life.

'The hammered anvils reel and chime;
  The breathless, belted wheels ring true;
The workmen join the ends of time,
  And forge and mould the world anew.'

A BALLAD OF TANNHÄUSER

'What hardy, tattered wretch is that
    Who on our Synod dares intrude?'
Pope Urban with his council sat,
    And near the door Tannhäuser stood.

His eye with light unearthly gleamed;
    His yellow hair hung round his head
In elf locks lusterless: he seemed
    Like one new-risen from the dead.

'Hear me, most Holy Father, tell
    The tale that burns my soul within.
I stagger on the brink of hell;
    No voice but yours can shrive my sin.'

'Speak, sinner.'   'From my father's house
    Lightly I stepped in haste for fame;
And hoped by deeds adventurous
    High on the world to carve my name.

'At early dawn I took my way;
    My heart with peals of gladness rang;
Nor could I leave the woods all day,
    Because the birds so sweetly sang.

' But when the happy birds had gone
    To rest, and night with panic fears
And blushes deep came stealing on,
    Another music thrilled my ears.

' I heard the evening wind serene,
    And all the wandering waters sing
The deep delight the day had been,
    The deep delight the night would bring.

' I heard the wayward earth express
    In one long-drawn melodious sigh
The rapture of the sun's caress,
    The passion of the brooding sky.

' The air, a harp of myriad chords,
    Intently murmured overhead;
My heart grew great with unsung words:
    I followed where the music led.

' It led me to a mountain-chain,
    Wherein athwart the deepening gloom,
High-hung above the wooded plain,
    Appeared a summit like a tomb.

' Aloft a giddy pathway wound
    That brought me to a darksome cave:
I heard, undaunted, underground
    Wild winds and wilder voices rave,

' And plunged into that stormy world.
    Cold hands assailed me impotent
In the gross darkness; serpents curled
    About my limbs; but on I went.

' The wild winds buffeted my face;
    The wilder voices shrieked despair;
A stealthy step with mine kept pace,
    And subtle terror steeped the air.

' But the sweet sound that throbbed on high
    Had left the upper world; and still
A cry rang in my heart—a cry!
    For lo, far in the hollow hill,

' The dulcet melody withdrawn
    Kept welling through the fierce uproar.
As I have seen the molten dawn
    Across a swarthy tempest pour,

' So suddenly the magic note,
    Transformed to light, a glittering brand,
Out of the storm and darkness smote
    A peaceful sky, a dewy land.

' I scarce could breathe, I might not stir,
    The while there came across the lea,
With singing maidens after her,
    A woman wonderful to see.

' Her face—her face was strong and sweet;
    Her looks were loving prophecies;
She kissed my brow: I kissed her feet—
    A woman wonderful to kiss.

She took me to a place apart
    Where eglantine and roses wove
A bower, and gave me all her heart—
    A woman wonderful to love.

' As I lay worshipping my bride,
    While rose leaves in her bosom fell,
And dreams came sailing on a tide
    Of sleep, I heard a matin bell.

' It beat my soul as with a rod
    Tingling with horror of my sin;
I thought of Christ, I thought of God,
    And of the fame I meant to win.

' I rose; I ran; nor looked behind;
    The doleful voices shrieked despair
In tones that pierced the crashing wind;
    And subtle terror warped the air.

' About my limbs the serpents curled;
    The stealthy step with mine kept pace;
But soon I reached the upper world:
    I sought a priest; I prayed for grace.

' He said, " Sad sinner, do you know
　　What fiend this is, the baleful cause
Of your dismay ? "　I loved her so
　　I never asked her what she was.

' He said, " Perhaps not God above
　　Can pardon such unheard-of ill:
It was the pagan Queen of Love
　　Who lured you to her haunted hill!

' " Each hour you spent with her was more
　　Than a full year!　Only the Pope
Can tell what heaven may have in store
　　For one who seems past help and hope."

' Forthwith I took the way to Rome:
　　I scarcely slept; I scarcely ate:
And hither quaking am I come,
　　But resolute to know my fate.

' Most Holy Father, save my soul!...
　　Ah God! again I hear the chime,
Sweeter than liquid bells that toll
　　Across a lake at vesper time ,...

' Her eyelids droop ... I hear her sigh . .
　　The roseleaves fall . . . . She falls asleep .
The cry rings in my blood—the cry
　　That surges from the deepest deep.

' No man was ever tempted so!—
    I say not this in my defence
Help, Father, help! or I must go!
    The dulcet music draws me hence!'

He knelt—he fell upon his face.
    Pope Urban said, ' The eternal cost
Of guilt like yours eternal grace
    Dare not remit : your soul is lost.

' When this dead staff I carry grows
    Again and blossoms, heavenly light
May shine on you.'   Tannhäuser rose;
    And all at once his face grew bright.

He saw the emerald leaves unfold,
    The emerald blossoms break and glance;
They watched him, wondering to behold
    The rapture of his countenance.

The undivined, eternal God
    Looked on him from the highest heaven,
And showed him by the budding rod
    There was no need to be forgiven.

He heard melodious voices call
    Across the world, an elfin shout;
And when he left the council-hall,
    It seemed a great light had gone out.

With anxious heart, with troubled brow,
    The Synod turned upon the Pope.
They saw; they cried, 'A living bough,
    A miracle, a pledge of hope!'

And Urban trembling saw: 'God's way
    Is not as man's,' he said.   'Alack!
Forgive me, gracious heaven, this day
    My sin of pride.   Go, bring him back.'

But swift as thought Tannhäuser fled,
    And was not found.   He scarcely slept;
He scarcely ate; for overhead
    The ceaseless, dulcet music kept

Wafting him on.   And evermore
    The foliate staff he saw at Rome
Pointed the way; and the winds bore
    Sweet voices whispering him to come.

The air, a world-enfolding flood
    Of liquid music poured along;
And the wild cry within his blood
    Became at last a golden song.

'All day,' he sang—'I feel all day
    The earth dilate beneath my feet;
I hear in fancy far away
    The tidal heart of ocean beat.

‘ My heart amasses as I run
    The depth of heaven's sapphire flower;
The resolute, enduring sun
    Fulfils my soul with splendid power.

‘ I quiver with divine desire;
    I clasp the stars; my thoughts immerse
Themselves in space; like fire in fire
    I melt into the universe.

‘ For I am running to my love:
    The eager roses burn below;
Orion wheels his sword above,
    To guard the way God bids me go.’

At dusk he reached the mountain chain,
    Wherein athwart the deepening gloom,
High hung above the wooded plain
    The Hörselberg rose like a tomb.

He plunged into the under-world;
    Cold hands assailed him impotent
In the gross darkness; serpents curled
    About his limbs; but on he went.

The wild winds buffeted his face;
    The wilder voices shrieked despair;
A stealthy step with his kept pace;
    And subtle terror steeped the air.

But once again the magic note,
  Transformed to light, a glittering brand,
Out of the storm and darkness smote
  A peaceful sky, a dewy land.

And once again he might not stir,
  The while there came across the lea
With singing maidens after her
  The Queen of Love so fair to see.

Her happy face was strong and sweet;
  Her looks were loving prophecies;
She kissed his brow; he kissed her feet—-
  He kissed the ground her feet did kiss.

She took him to a place apart
  Where eglantine and roses wove
A bower, and gave him all her heart—
  The Queen of Love, the Queen of Love.

As he lay worshipping his bride
  While rose-leaves in her bosom fell,
And dreams came sailing on a tide
  Of sleep, he heard a matin-bell.

'Hark! Let us leave the magic hill,'
  He said, 'And live on earth with men.'
'No; here,' she said, 'we stay, until
  The Golden Age shall come again.'

And so they wait, while empires sprung
    Of hatred thunder past above,
Deep in the earth for ever young
    Tannhäuser and the Queen of Love.

A BALLAD OF EUTHANASIA

In magic books she read at night,
  And found all things to be
A spectral pageant brought to light
  By nameless sorcery.

‘ Bethink you, now, my daughter dear,’
  The King of Norway cried,
‘ ’Tis summer, and your twentieth year—
  High time you were a bride!

‘ The sunlight lingers o’er the wold
  By night; the stars above
With passion throb like hearts of gold;
  The whole world is in love.’

The scornful princess laughed and said,
  ‘ This love you praise, I hate.
Oh, I shall never, never wed;
  For men degenerate.

‘ The sun grows dim on heaven’s brow;
  The world’s worn blood runs cold;
Time staggers in his dotage now;
  Nature is growing old.

‘ Deluded by the summertime,
    Must I with wanton breath
Whisper and sigh? I trow not!—I
    Shall be the bride of Death.’

Fair princes came with gems of price,
    And kings from lands afar.
‘ Jewels!’ she said. ‘ I may not wed
    Till Death comes with a star.’

At midnight when she ceased to read,
    She pushed her lattice wide,
And saw the crested rollers lead
    The vanguard of the tide.

The mighty host of waters swayed,
    Commanded by the moon;
The wind a marching music made;
    The surges chimed in tune.

But she with sudden-startled ears
    O’erheard a ghostly sound—
Or drums that beat, or trampling feet,
    Above or underground.

The mountain-side was girt about
    With forests dark and deep.
‘ What meteor flashes in and out
    Thridding the darksome steep ?’

Soon light and sound reached level ground,
And lo, in blackest mail,
Along the shore a warrior
Rode on a war-horse pale!

And from his helm as on he came
A crescent lustre gleamed;
The charger's hoofs were shod with flame:
The wet sand hissed and steamed.

' He leaves me!   Nay; he turns this way
From elfin lands afar.
' 'Tis Death,' she said.   ' He comes to wed
His true love with a star!

' No ring for me, no blushing groom,
No love with all its ills,
No long-drawn life!   I am the wife
Of Death, whose first kiss kills.'

The rider reached the city wall;
Over the gate he dashed;
Across the roofs the fire-shod hoofs
Like summer-lightning flashed.

Before her bower the pale horse pawed
The air, unused to rest;
The sable groom, he whispered ' Come!'
And stooped his shining crest.

She sprang behind him; on her brow ✗
   He placed his glowing star.
Back o'er the roofs the fire-shod hoofs `
   Like lightning flashed afar.

Through hissing sand and shrivelled grass
   And flowers singed and dead,
By wood and lea, by stream and sea,
   The pale horse panting sped.

At last as they beheld the morn
   His sovereignty resume,
Deep in an ancient land forlorn
   They reached a marble tomb.

They lighted down and entered in: ‹
   The tears, they brimmed her eyes;   /
She turned and took a lingering look, ⤴
   A last look at the skies;

Then went with Death.   Her lambent star ⤴
   The sullen darkness lit
In avenues of sombre yews,   ′
   Where ghosts did peer and flit.

But soon the way grew light as day; ⤴
   With wonderment and awe,
A golden land, a silver strand,
   And grass-green hills she saw.

In gown and smock good country folk
  In fields and meadows worked;
The salt seas wet the ruddy net
  Where glistering fishes lurked.

The meads were strewn with purple flowers,
  With every flower that blows;
And singing loud o'er cliff and cloud,
  The larks, the larks arose!

' The sun is bright on heaven's brow,
  The world's fresh blood runs fleet;
Time is as young as ever now,
  Nature as fresh and sweet,'

Her champion said; then through the wood
  He led her to a bower;
He doffed his sable casque and stood
  A young man in his flower!

' Lo! I am Life, your lover true!'
  He kissed her o'er and o'er.
And still she wist not what to do,
  And still she wondered more.

And they were wed. The swift years sped
  Till children's children laughed;
And joy and pain and joy again
  Mixed in the cup they quaffed.

Upon their golden wedding day,
  He said, 'How now, dear wife?'
Then she: 'I find the sweetest kind
  Of Death is Love and Life.'

A BALLAD OF A COWARD

THE trumpets pealed; the echoes sang
  A tossing fugue; before it died,
Again the rending trumpets rang,
  Again the phantom notes replied.

In galleries, on straining roofs,
  At once ten thousand tongues were hushed
When down the lists a storm of hoofs
  From either border thundering rushed.

A knight whose arms were chased and set
  With gold and gems, in fear withdrew
Before the fronts of tourney met,
  Before the spears in splinters flew.

He reached the wilds. He cast away
  His lance and shield and arms of price;
He turned his charger loose, and lay
  Face-downwards in his cowardice.

His wife had seen the recreant fly:
  She followed, found, and called his name.
‘ Sweetheart, I will not have you die:
  My love,’ she said, ‘can heal your shame.’

Not long his vanity withstood
   Her gentleness.   He left his soul
To her; and her solicitude,
   He being a coward, made him whole.

Yet was he blessed in heart and head;
   Forgiving; of his riches free;
Wise was he too, and deeply read,
   And ruled his earldom righteously.

A war broke out.   With fateful speed
   The foe, eluding watch and ward,
Conquered; and none was left to lead
   The land, save this faint-hearted lord.

' Here is no shallow tournament,
   No soulless, artificial fight.
Courageously, in deep content,
   I go to combat for the right.'

The hosts encountered: trumpets spoke;
   Drums called aloud; the air was torn
With cannon, light by stifling smoke
   Estopped, and shrieking battle born.

But he ?—he was not in the van!
   The vision of his child and wife ?
Even that deserted him.   He ran—
   The coward ran to save his life.

The lowliest men would sooner face
   A thousand dreadful deaths, than come
Before their loved ones in disgrace;
   Yet this sad coward hurried home:

For, as he fled, his cunning heart
   Declared he might be happy yet
In some retreat where Love and Art
   Should swathe his soul against regret.

' My wife! my son!   For their dear sakes,'
   He thought, ' I save myself by flight.'—
He reached his place.   ' What comet shakes
   Its baleful tresses on the night

Above my towers ? '   Alas, the foe
   Had been before with sword and fire!
His loved ones in their blood lay low:
   Their dwelling was their funeral pyre.

Then he betook him to a hill
   Which in his happy times had been
His silent friend, meaning to kill
   Himself upon its bosom green.

But an old mood at every tread
   Returned; and with assured device
The wretched coward's cunning head
   Distilled it into cowardice.

' A snowy owl on silent wings
   Sweeps by; and, ah! I know the tune
The wayward night-wind sweetly sings
   And dreaming birds in coverts croon.

' The cocks their muffled catches crow;
   The river ripples dark and bright;
I hear the pastured oxen low,
   And the whole rumour of the night.

' The moon comes from the wind-swept hearth
   Of heaven; the stars beside her soar;
The seas and harvests of the earth
   About her shadowy footsteps pour.

' But though remembrances, all wet
   With happy tears, their tendrils coil
Close round my heart; though I be set
   And rooted in the ruddy soil,

' My pulses with the planets leap;
   The veil is rent before my face;
My aching nerves are mortised deep
   In furthest cavities of space;

' Through the pervading ether speed
   My thoughts that now the stars rehearse;
And should I take my life, the deed
   Would disarray the universe.'

Gross cowardice!   Hope, while we breathe,
　　Can make the meanest prize his breath,
And still with starry garlands wreathe
　　The nakedness of life and death.

He wandered vaguely for a while;
　　Then thought at last to hide his shame
And self-contempt far in an isle
　　Among the outer deeps; but came,

Even there, upon a seaboard dim,
　　Where like the slowly ebbing tide
That weltered on the ocean's rim
　　With sanguine hues of sunset dyed,

The war still lingered.   Suddenly,
　　Ere he could run, the bloody foam
Of battle burst about him; he,
　　Scarce knowing what he did, struck home,

As those he helped began to fly,
　　Bidding him follow. ‘Nay,’ he said;
‘ Nay; I die fighting—even I!’
　　And happy and amazed fell dead.

A BALLAD OF LANCELOT

By coasts where scalding deserts reek,
  The apanages of despair;
In outland wilds, by firth and creek,
  O'er icy bournes of silver air;

In storm or calm delaying not,
  To every noble task addressed,
Year after year, Sir Lancelot
  Fulfilled King Arthur's high behest.

He helped the helpless ones; withstood
  Tyrants and sanctioners of vice;
He rooted out the dragon brood,
  And overthrew false deities.

Alone with his own soul, alone
  With life and death, with day and night,
His thought and strength grew great and shone
  A tongue of flame, a sword of light.

And yet not all alone.   On high,
  When midnight set the spaces free,
And brimming stars hung from the sky
  Low down, and spilt their jewellery,

Behind the nightly squandered fire,
  Through a dark lattice only seen
By love, a look of rapt desire
  Fell from a vision of the Queen.

From heaven she bent when twilight knit
  The dusky air and earth in one;
He saw her like a goddess sit
  Enthroned upon the noonday sun.

In passages of gulfs and sounds,
  When wild winds dug the sailor's grave,
When clouds and billows merged their bounds,
  And the keel climbed the slippery wave,

A sweet sigh laced the tempest; nay,
  Low at his ear he heard her speak;
Among the hurtling sheaves of spray
  Her loosened tresses swept his cheek.

And in the revelry of death,
  If human greed of slaughter cast
Remorse aside, a violet breath,
  The incense of her being passed

Across his soul, and deeply swayed
  The fount of pity; o'er the strife
He curbed the lightning of his blade,
  And gave the foe his forfeit life.

Low on the heath, or on the deck,
　　In bloody mail or wet with brine,
Asleep he saw about her neck
　　The wreath of gold and rubies shine;

He saw her brows, her lovelit face,
　　And on her cheek one passionate tear;
He felt in dreams the rich embrace,
　　The beating heart of Guinevere.

' Visions that haunt my couch, my path,
　　Although the waste, unfathomed sea
Should rise against me white with wrath
　　I must behold her verily,

' Once ere I die,' he said, and turned
　　Westward his faded silken sails
From isles where cloudy mountains burned,
　　And north to Severn-watered Wales.

Beside the Usk King Arthur kept
　　His Easter court, a glittering rout.
But Lancelot, because there swept
　　A passion of despair throughout

His being, when he saw once more
　　The sky that canopied, the tide
That girdled Guinevere, forbore
　　His soul's desire, and wandered wide

In unknown seas companionless,
   Eating his heart, until by chance
He drifted into Lyonesse,
   The wave-worn kingdom of romance.

He leapt ashore and watched his barque
   Unmastered stagger to its doom;
Then doffed his arms and fled baresark
   Into the forest's beckoning gloom.

The exceeding anguish of his mind
   Had broken him.   'King Arthur's trust,'
He cried; 'ignoble, fateful, blind!
   Her love and my love, noxious lust!

'Dupes of our senses!   Let us eat
   In caverns fathoms underground,
Alone, ashamed!   To sit at meat
   In jocund throngs?—the most profound

'Device of life the mountebank,
   Vendor of gilded ashes!   Steal
From every sight to use the rank
   And loathsome needs that men conceal;

'And crush and drain in curtained beds
   The clusters called of love; but feed
With garlanded uplifted heads;
   Invite the powers that sanction greed

' To countenance the revel; boast
    Of hunger, thirst; be drunken; claim
Indulgence to the uttermost,
    Replenishing the founts of shame!'

He gathered berries, efts, and snails,
    Sorrel, and new-burst hawthorn leaves;
Uprooted with his savage nails
    Earth-nuts; and under rocky eaves

Shamefast devoured them, out of sight
    In darkness, lest the eye of beast,
Or bird, or star, or thing of night
    Uncouth, unknown, should watch him feast.

At noon in twilight depths of pine
    He heard the word Amaimon spoke;
He saw the pallid, evil sign
    The wred-eld lit upon the oak.

The viper loitered in his way;
    The minx looked up with bloodshot leer;
Ill-meaning fauns and lamiæ
    With icy laughter flitted near.

But if he came upon a ring
    Of sinless elves, and crept unseen
Beneath the brake to hear them sing,
    And watch them dancing on the green,

They touched earth with their finger-tips;
   They ceased their roundelay; they laid
A seal upon their elfin lips
   And vanished in the purple shade.

At times he rent the dappled flank
   Of some fair creature of the chase,
Mumbled its flesh, or growling drank
   From the still-beating heart, his face

And jowl ruddled, and in his hair
   And beard, blood-painted straws and burs,
While eagles barked screening the air,
   And wolves that were his pensioners.

Sometimes at night his mournful cry
   Troubled all waking things; the mole
Dived to his deepest gallery;
   The vixen from the moonlit knoll

Passed like a shadow underground,
   And the mad satyr in his lair
Whined bodeful at the world-old sound
   Of inarticulate despair.

Sir Lancelot, beloved of men!
   The ancient earth gat hold of him;
A year was blotted from his ken
   In the enchanted forest dim.

At Easter when the thorn beset
    The bronzing wood with silver sprays,
And hyacinth and violet
    Empurpled all the russet ways;

When buttercup and daffodil
    A stainless treasure-trove unrolled,
And cowslips had begun to fill
    Their chalices with sweeter gold,

He heard a sound of summer rush
    By swarthy grove and kindled lawn;
He heard, he sighed to hear the thrush
    Singing alone before the dawn.

Forward he stalked with eyes on fire
    Like one who keeps in sound and sight
An angel with celestial lyre
    Descanting rapturous delight.

He left behind the spell-bound wood;
    He saw the branchless air unfurled;
He climbed a hill and trembling stood
    Above the prospect of the world.

With lustre in its bosom pent
    From many a shining summer day
And harvest moon, the wan sea leant
    Against a heaven of iron-grey.

Inland on the horizon beat
    And flickered, drooping heavily,
A fervid haze, a vaporous heat,
    The dusky eyelid of the sky.

White ways, white gables, russet thatch
    Fretted the green and purple plain;
The herd undid his woven latch;
    The bleating flock went forth again;

The skylarks uttered lauds and prime;
    The sheep-bells rang from hill to hill;
The cuckoo pealed his mellow chime;
    The orient bore a burden shrill.

His memory struggled half awake;
    Dimly he groped within to see
What star, what sun, what light should break
    And set his darkened spirit free.

But from without deliverance came:
    Afar he saw a horseman speed,
A knight, a spirit clad in flame
    Riding upon a milkwhite steed.

For now the sun had quenched outright
    The clouds and all their working charms,
Marshalled his legionary light,
    And fired the rider's golden arms.

Softly the silver billows flowed;
    Beneath the hill the emerald vale
Dipped seaward; on the burnished road
    The milkwhite steed, the dazzling mail

Advanced and flamed against the wind;
    And Lancelot, his body rent
With the fierce trial of his mind
    To know, reeled down the steep descent.

Remembrances of battle plied
    His soul with ruddy beams of day.
' A horse! a lance! to arms!' he cried,
    And stood there weeping in the way.

' Speak!' said the knight. 'What man are you?'
    ' I know not yet. Surely of old
I rode in arms, and fought and slew
    In jousts and battles manifold.'

Oh, wistfully he drew anear,
    Fingered the reins, the jewelled sheath;
With rigid hand he grasped the spear,
    And shuddering whispered, ' Life and death,

' Love, lofty deeds, renown—did these
    Attend me once in days unknown ? '
With courtesy, with comely ease,
    And brows that like his armour shone,

The golden knight dismounting took
　　Sir Lancelot by the hand and said,
‘ Your voice of woe, your lonely look
　　As of a dead man whom the dead

‘ Themselves cast out—whence are they, friend ?’
　　Sir Lancelot a moment hung
In doubt, then knelt and made an end
　　Of all his madness, tensely strung

In one last effort to be free
　　Of evil things that wait for men
In secret, strangle memory,
　　And shut the soul up in their den.

‘ Spirit,’ he said, ‘ I know your eyes:
　　They bridge with light the heavy drift
Of years. . . . A woman said, “ Arise;
　　And if you love the Queen, be swift! ”

‘ The token was an emerald chased
　　In gold, once mine. Wherefore I rode
At dead of night in proudest haste
　　To Payarne where the Queen abode.

‘ A crafty witch gave me to drink:
　　Almost till undern of the morn
Silent, in darkness. . . . When I think
　　It was not Guinevere, self-scorn

‘ Cuts to the marrow of my bones,
  A blade of fire. Can wisdom yield
No mood, no counsel, that atones
  For wasted love! . . . Heaven had revealed

‘ That she should bear a child to me
  My bed-mate said. . . . Yet am I mad
The offspring of that treachery!
  The maiden knight! You—Galahad,

‘ My son, who make my trespass dear!’
  His look released his father's thought—
The darkling orbs of Guinevere;
  For so had Lancelot's passion wrought.

With tenderer tears than women shed
  Sir Galahad held his father fast.
‘ Now I shall be your squire,’ he said.
  But Lancelot fought him long. At last

The maiden gently overpowered
  The man. Upon his milkwhite steed
He brought him where a castle towered
  Midmost a green enamelled mead;

And clothed his body, clothed his heart
  In human garniture once more.
‘ My father, bid me now depart.
  I hear beside the clanging shore,

E

' Above the storm, or in the wind,
    Outland, or on the old Roman street,
  A chord of music intertwined
    From wandering tones deep-hued and sweet.

' Afar or near, at noon, at night,
    The braided sound attends and fills
  My soul with peace, as heaven with light
    O'erflows when morning crowns the hills.

' And with the music, seen or hid,
    A blood-rose on the palace lawn,
  A fount of crimson, dark amid
    The stains and glories of the dawn;

' Above the city's earthly hell
    A token ominous of doom,
  A cup on fire and terrible
    With thunders in its ruddy womb;

' But o'er the hamlet's fragrant smoke,
    The dance and song at eventide,
  A beating heart, the gentle yoke
    Of life the bridegroom gives the bride;

' A ruby shadow on the snow;
    A flower, a lamp— through every veil
  And mutable device I know,
    And follow still the Holy Grail

' Until God gives me my new name
    Empyreal, and the quest be done.'
Then like a spirit clad in flame,
    He kissed his father and was gone.

Long gazed Sir Lancelot on the ground
    Tormented till benign repose
Enveloped him in depths profound
    Of sweet oblivion.   When he rose

The bitterest was past.   ' And I
    Shall follow now the Holy Grail,
Seen, or unseen, until I die:
    My very purpose shall avail

' My soul,' he said.   By day, by night
    He rode abroad, his vizor up;
With sun and moon his vehement sight
    Fought for a vision of the cup—

In vain.   For evermore on high
    When darkness set the spaces free,
And brimming stars hung from the sky
    Low down, and spilt their jewellery,

Behind the nightly squandered fire,
    Through a dim lattice only seen
By love, a look of rapt desire
    Fell from a vision of the Queen.

From heaven she bent when twilight knit
   The dusky air and earth in one;
He saw her like a goddess sit
   Enthroned upon the noonday sun.

Wherefore he girt himself again:
   In lawless towns and savage lands,
He overthrew unrighteous men,
   Accomplishing the King's commands.

In passages of gulfs and sounds
   When wild winds dug the sailor's grave,
When clouds and billows merged their bounds,
   And the keel climbed the slippery wave,

A sweet sigh laced the tempest; nay,
   Low at his ear he heard her speak;
Among the hurtling sheaves of spray
   Her loosened tresses swept his cheek.

And in the revelry of death,
   If human greed of slaughter cast
Remorse aside, a violet breath,
   The incense of her being passed

Across his soul, and deeply swayed
   The fount of pity; o'er the strife
He curbed the lightning of his blade,
   And gave the foe his forfeit life.

His love, in utter woe annealed,
   Escaped the furnace, sweet and clear—
His love that on the world had sealed
   The look, the soul of Guinevere.

A BALLAD IN BLANK VERSE

His father's house looked out across a firth
Broad-bosomed like a mere, beside a town
Far in the North, where Time could take his ease,
And Change hold holiday; where Old and New
Weltered upon the border of the world.

'Oh now,' he thought—a youth whose sultry eyes,
Bold brow and wanton mouth were not all lust,
But haunted from within and from without
By memories, visions, hopes, divine desires—
'Now may my life beat out upon this shore
A prouder music than the winds and waves
Can compass in their haughtiest moods.   I need
No world more spacious than the region here:
The foam-embroidered firth, a purple path
For argosies that still on pinions speed,
Or fiery-hearted cleave with iron limbs
And bows precipitous the pliant sea;
The sloping shores that fringe the velvet tides
With heavy bullion and with golden lace
Of restless pebble woven and fine spun sand;

The villages that sleep the winter through,
And, wakening with the spring, keep festival
All summer and all autumn: this grey town
That pipes the morning up before the lark
With shrieking steam, and from a hundred stalks
Lacquers the sooty sky; where hammers clang
On iron hulls, and cranes in harbours creak
Rattle and swing, whole cargoes on their necks;
Where men sweat gold that others hoard or spend,
And lurk like vermin in their narrow streets:
This old grey town, this firth, the further strand
Spangled with hamlets, and the wooded steeps,
Whose rocky tops behind each other press,
Fantastically carved like antique helms
High-hung in heaven's cloudy armoury,
Is world enough for me.   Here daily dawn
Burns through the smoky east; with fire-shod feet
The sun treads heaven, and steps from hill to hill
Downward before the night that still pursues
His crimson wake; here winter plies his craft,
Soldering the years with ice; here spring appears,
Caught in a leafless brake, her garland torn,
Breathless with wonder, and the tears half-dried
Upon her rosy cheek; here summer comes
And wastes his passion like a prodigal
Right royally; and here her golden gains
Free-handed as a harlot autumn spends;
And here are men to know, women to love.'

His father, woman-hearted, great of soul,
Wilful and proud, save for one little shrine
That held a pinch-beck cross, had closed and barred
The many mansions of his intellect.

'My son,' he said—to him, fresh from his firth
And dreams at evening; while his mother sat,
She also with her dingy crucifix
And feeble rushlight, praying for her boy—
'My son, have you decided for the Lord?
Your mother's heart and mine are exercised
For your salvation.   Will you turn to Christ?
Now, young and strong, you hanker for the world;
But think: the longest life must end at last,
And then come Death and Judgment.   Are you fit
To meet your God before the great white throne?
If on the instant Death should summon you,
What doom would the Eternal Judge pronounce—
'Depart from me,' or 'Sit on My right hand?'
In life it is your privilege to choose,
But after death you have no choice at all.
Die unbelieving, and in endless woe
You must believe throughout eternity.
My son, reject not Christ; he pleads through me;
The Holy Spirit uses my poor words.
How it would fill your mother's heart and mine,
And God's great heart with joy unspeakable,
Were you, a helpless sinner, now to cry,

'Lord I believe: help Thou mine unbelief.'
He clenched his teeth; his blood, fulfilled of brine,
Of sunset, and his dreams, boomed in his ears.
A vision rose before him; and the sound
Husky and plaintive of his father's voice
Seemed unintelligible and afar.
He saw Apollo on the Dardan beach:
The waves lay still; the winds hung motionless,
And held their breath to hear the rebel god,
Conquered and doomed, with stormy sobbing song,
And crashing discords of his golden lyre,
Reluctantly compel the walls of Troy,
Unquarried and unhewn, in supple lines
And massive strength to rise about the town.

A quavering voice shattered his fantasy:
His father's pleading done, his mother cried,
With twitching forehead, scalding tears that broke
The seal of wrinkled eyelids, mortised hands
Where knuckles jutted white: 'Almighty God!—
Almighty God!—Oh, save my foolish boy.'

He glanced about the dreary parlour, clenched
His teeth, and once again his blood, fulfilled
Of brine, of sunset, and his dreams, exhaled
A vision.   While his parents clutched their hearts,
Expecting his conversion instantly,
And listened if perchance they might o'erhear

The silent heavens burst into applause
Over one lost repentant, he beheld
The Cyprian Aphrodite, all one blush
And glance of passion, from the violet sea
Step inland, fastening as she went her zone.
She reached a gulf that opened in the ground
Deep in a leafless wood and waited there,
Battling the darkness with her wistful eyes.
Then suddenly she blanched and blushed again,
And her divinely pulsing body bowed
With outstretched arms over the yawning earth.
Straightway Adonis, wonderstruck and pale,
Stole from the sepulchre, a moonbeam wraith.
But Aphrodite with a golden cry
That echoed round the world and shook the stars,
Caught him and thawed him in her warm embrace,
And murmuring kisses bore him to her bower.
Then all the trees were lit with budding flames
Of emerald, and all the meads and leas,
Coverts and shady places, glades and dells,
Odoured and dimly stained with opening flowers,
And loud with love-songs of impassioned birds,
Became the shrine and hostel of the spring.

His wanton face grew sweet and wonderful,
Beholding Aphrodite.   But they thought—
His father and his mother, sick with hope—
It was the Holy Ghost's effectual call.

Entranced he rose and glided from the room;
They, undeceived, like little children sobbed.

Slowly he broke his mother's tender heart,
Until she died in anguish for his sins.
His father then besought him on his knees,
With tears and broken speech and pleading hands

' My son,' he said, ' you open all the wounds
Daily and nightly of the Lord of Heaven:
You killed your mother, you are killing me:
Is it not sin enough, poor foolish boy ? '

For this was in the North, where Time stands still
And Change holds holiday, where Old and New
Welter upon the border of the world,
And savage faith works woe.

     ' Oh, let me be!'
The dreamer cried, and rushing from the house
He sought the outcast Aphrodite, dull,
Tawdry, unbeautiful, but still divine
Even in the dark streets of a noisome port.

At times he wrote his dreams, rebellious still
That he should be constrained to please himself
As one is eased by roaring on the rack.
Desperate he grew, and wandering by his firth,

Exclaimed against the literature he loved.
'Lies, lies!' he muttered.   'And the noblest, lies!
Why should we lie? what penalty is this—
To write, and sing, and think, and speculate,
Hag-ridden by ideas, or 'twixt the shafts
Like broken horses, blinded, bitted, reined,
And whipped about the world by steel-tagged creeds!'

Wasted and sad with wantonness, and wan
With fantasy—a furnace seven times hot,
Wherein he tried all things; and wrung with woe
To see his father dying for his sake,
And by the memory of his mother's death,
He yielded tamely and professed himself
Convinced of sin but confident in Christ.

Then to the table of the Lord he went,
Ghastly, with haunted eyes that shone, and limbs
That scarcely bore him, like a heretic
Led to the chamber where tormentors stood
Muffled and silent, earnest to explore,
With cunning flames and cords and engines dire,
The sunken wells of pain, the gloomy gulfs
Obscurely wallowing in the souls of men.

In solemn tones the grey-haired presbyter—
'This is My body which is given for you,
This do in memory of Me.'

The boy,

Whose blood within him clamoured like a storm,
Uttered a smothered cry and rose, but lo!
The happy triumph on his father's face!
'Why do I not die now? like husks of corn,
The bread, like vitriol the sip of wine!
I eat and drink damnation to myself
To give my father's troubled spirit peace.'
The stealthy elders creaked about the floor,
Guiding the cup and platter; looking down,
The children in the gallery smirked and watched
Who took the deepest draught; and ancient dames
Crumpled their folded handerchiefs, and pressed
With knuckly fingers sprays of southernwood.

Ah! down no silver beam the Holy Grail
Glided from Heaven, a crimson cup that throbbed
As throbs the heart divine; no aching sounds
Of scarce-heard music stole into the aisle,
Like disembodied pulses beating love.

But in the evening by the purple firth
He walked, and saw brown locks upon the brine,
And pale hands beckon him to come away,
Where mermaids, with their harps and golden combs,
Sit throned upon the carven antique poops
Of treasure-ships, and soft sea-dirges sing
Over the green-gilt bones of mariners.

He saw vast forms and dreadful draw aside
The flowing crimson curtains of the west
With far-off thundrous rustle, and threaten him
From heaven's porch; beneath his feet the earth
Quaked like a flame-sapped bridge that spans the wave
Of fiery Phlegethon; and in the wind
An icy voice was borne from some waste place,
Piercing him to the marrow.   Night came down,
And still he wandered helpless by the firth,
That under clouded skies gleamed black and smooth
Like cooling pitch.   But when the moon broke out
And poured athwart the glittering ebony
Torrents of molten silver, hurtling thoughts
Trooped forth disorderly.

                              ' I'll have no creed,
He said.   ' Though I be weakest of my kind,
I'll have no creed.   Lo! there is but one creed,
The vulture-phœnix that for ever tears
The soul of man in chains of flesh and blood
Rivetted to the earth; the clime, the time,
Change but its plumage.   Gluttonous bird of prey,
More fatal than all famines, plagues and wars,
I wrench you off, although my soul go too!
With bloody claws and dripping beak unfleshed,
Spread out your crackling vans that darken heaven;
Rabid and curst, fly yelping where you list!
Henceforth I shall be God; for consciousness

Is God: I suffer; I am God: this Self,
That all the universe combines to quell,
Is greater than the universe; and *I*
Am that I am.   To think and not be God ?—
It cannot be!   Lo! I shall spread this news,
And gather to myself a band of Gods—
An army, and go forth against the world,
Conquering and to conquer.   Snowy steppes
Of Muscovy, frost-bound Siberian plains,
And scalding sands of Ethiopia,
Where groans oppress the bosom of the wind,
And men in gangs are driven to icy graves,
Or lashed to brutish slavery under suns
Whose sheer beams scorch and flay like burning blades,
Shall ring, enfranchised, with divine delight.
At home, where millions mope, in labyrinths
Of hideous streets astray without a clue,
Unfed, unsexed, unsoulled, unhelped, I bring
Life, with the gospel, " Up, quit you like Gods!''

Possessed with this, upon his father's hour
Of new-found happiness he burst, and cried,
' Father, my father, I have news to tell!
I know the word that shall uproot the thrones
Of oldest monarchs, and for ever lay
The doting phantom with the triple crown:
A word dynamic with the power of doom
To blast conventicles and parliaments,

Unsolder federations, crumble states,
And in the fining pot cast continents.
A word that shall a new beginning be,
And out of chaos make the world again.
Behold, my father! we, who heretofore,
Fearful and weak, deep-dyed in Stygian creeds
Against the shafts of pain and woe, have walked
The throbbing earth, most vulnerable still
In every pore and nerve: we, trembling things,
Who but an hour ago in frantic dread
Burned palsied women, and with awe beheld
A shaven pate mutter a latin spell
Over a biscuit: we, even we are Gods!
Nothing beneath, about us, or above
Is higher than ourselves.   Henceforth degree,
Authority, religion, government,
Employer and employed are obsolete
As penal torture or astrology.
The mighty spirit of the universe,
Conscious in us, shall ' . . .

                              Suddenly aware
Of gaping horror on his father's face,
He paused; and he, the old man, white as death,
With eyes like stars upon the crack of doom,
Rose quaking; and ' The unpardonable sin!—
The unpardonable sin!' he whispered hoarse.
' This was the sin of Lucifer—to make

Himself God's equal.   If I may, my son—
If it be God's will, I shall go to hell
To be beside you.   I shall be there first:
I have not many hours to live.   I thought—
Here as I sat beside your mother's chair—
I—my boy!—I wander somewhat.   Let me—
I'll sit again.—Let me remember now
How happy I have been to-day, my son
A member of the Church of Christ, and I
Beside him at Communion, seeing him
And seeing at the window of heaven the face
Of her who bore him, sweet and glorified.
At home I sit and think that, as he lived
Most absolute in sin, he shall, like Paul
Be as insatiable in doing well.
I think how, when my time comes, I shall go
And tell his mother of his holy life
Of labour for the Lord; and then I see
My boy at last appear before the Throne.
"By what right com'st thou here?" the Judge de-
        mands.
He hangs his head; but round about him throng
A crowd of souls, who cry "He was our staff;
He led us here."   "Sit thou on My right hand,"
The sentence falls; and we, my wife and I,
Awaiting you. . . .   There came a devil in
Wearing the likeness of my boy, and said
He was predestined for a reprobate,

A special vessel of the wrath of God.
Holy he was begotten; holy born;
With tearful prayers attended all his life;
Cherished with scrupulous love, and shown the path
To heaven by her who ne'er shall see him there;
For out of this there comes but blasphemy
And everlasting Hell. . . .   Ah! who are these?
My soul is hustled by a multitude
Of wild-eyed prodigals and wrenched about.
Boy, help me to blaspheme.   I cannot face
Without you her that nursed you at her breast.
Let us curse God together and going forth
Plunge headlong in the waves, and be at rest
In Hell for evermore.   Some end to this!—
This awful gnawing pain in every part!
Or certainty that this will never end!
This, now, is Hell! . . .   There was a paltry way
Of fooling God some casuists hit upon.
How went it?   Yes, that God did fore-ordain
And so foreknew that those who should believe
Should enter glory of their own free-will.
Ah! pink of blasphemies that makes of God
An impotent spectator!   Let us two
Believe in this, and that shall damn us best! . .
I dare, but cannot; for the Lord of Hosts,
The God of my salvation, is my God:
He, ere the world began, predestined me
To life eternal : to the bitter end

Against my will I persevere, a saint;
And find my will at length the will of God.
What is my son, and what the hopes and fears
Of my dead wife and me before the flame
Of God's pure purpose, His, from whose dread eyes
The earth and heaven fled and found no place!
Beside the crystal river I shall walk
For ever with the Lord   The city of gold,
The jasper walls thereof, the gates of pearl,
The bright foundation-stones of emerald,
Of sapphire, chrysoprase, of every gem,
And the high triumph of unending day
Shall be but wildfire on a summer eve
Beside the exceeding glory of delight,
That shall entrance me with the constant thought
Of how in Hell through all eternity
My son performs the perfect will of God.
Amen.   I come, Lord Jesus.   If his sin
Be not to death   . Heaven opens!' .

                Thus he died;
For this was in the North where Time stands still,
And Change holds holiday; where Old and New
Welter upon the border of the world,
And savage creeds can kill.

                The trembling boy
Knelt down, but dared to think, ' A dreadful death!

To die believing in so dull a God,
A useless Hell, a jewel-huckster's Heaven!'
Forthwith it flashed like light across his mind,
' If it be terrible into the hands
Of the living God to fall, how much more dire
To sicken face to face, like our sad age,
Chained to an icy corpse of deity,
Decked though it be and painted and embalmed!'

He took his father's hand and kissed his brow
And, weeping like a woman, watched him long;
Then softly rose and stepped into the night.
He stood beside the house a little space,
Hearing the wind speak low in whispers quaint,
An irresponsible and wandering voice.
But soon he hastened to the water's edge;
For from the shore there came sea-minstrelsy
Of waves that broke upon the hollow beach,
With liquid sound of pearling surges blent,
Cymbals, and muffled drums and dulcimers.

Sparse diamonds in the dead-black dome of night,
A few stars lit the moon-deserted air
And swarthy heaving of the firth obscure.
He, knowing every rock and sandy reach,
All night unfalteringly walked the shore,
While tempest after tempest rose and fell
Within his soul, that like an o'er-wrought sea

Laboured to burst its continent and hang
Some glittering trophy high among the stars.
At last the fugal music of the tide,
With cymbals, muffled drums, and dulcimers,
Into his blood a rhythmic measure beat,
And gave his passion scope and way in words.

' How unintelligent, how blind am I,
How vain!' he cried   ' A God ? a mole, a worm!
An engine frail, of brittle bones conjoined;
With tissue packed; with nerves, transmitting force;
And driven by water, thick and coloured red:
That may for some few pence a day be hired
In thousands to be shot at!   Oh, a God,
That lies and steals and murders!   Such a God
Passionate, dissolute, incontinent!
A God that starves in thousands, and ashamed,
Or shameless in the workhouse lurks; that sweats
In mines and foundries!   An enchanted God,
Whose nostrils in a palace breathe perfume,
Whose cracking shoulders hold the palace up,
Whose shoeless feet are rotting in the mire!
A God who said a little while ago,
'' I'll have no creed; '' and of his Godhood straight
Patched up a creed unwittingly—with which
He went and killed his father.   Subtle lie
That tempts our weakness always; magical,
And magically changed to suit the time!

" Lo, ye shall be as Gods! "—the serpent's cry—
Rose up again, " Ye shall be sons of God; "
And now the glosing word is in the air,
" Thou shalt be God by simply taking thought."
And if one could, believing this, convert
A million to be upright, chaste and strong,
Gentle and tolerant, it were but to found
A new religion, bringing new offence,
Setting the child against the father still.
Some thought imprisons us; we set about
To bring the world within the woven spell:
Our ruthless creeds that bathe the earth in blood
Are moods by alchemy made dogmas of—
The petrifaction of a metaphor.
No creed for me! I am a man apart:
A mouthpiece for the creeds of all the world;
A soulless life that angels may possess
Or demons haunt, wherein the foulest things
May loll at ease beside the loveliest;
A martyr for all mundane moods to tear;
The slave of every passion; and the slave
Of heat and cold, of darkness and of light;
A trembling lyre for every wind to sound.
I am a man set by to overhear
The inner harmony, the very tune
Of Nature's heart; to be a thoroughfare
For all the pageantry of Time; to catch
The mutterings of the Spirit of the Hour

And make them known; and of the lowliest
To be the minister, and therefore reign
Prince of the powers of the air, lord of the world
And master of the sea.   Within my heart
I'll gather all the universe, and sing
As sweetly as the spheres; and I shall be
The first of men to understand himself. ;
And lo! to give me courage comes the dawn,
Crimsoning the smoky east; and still the sun '
With fire-shod feet shall step from hill to hill
Downward before the night; winter shall ply
His ancient craft, soldering the years with ice;
And spring appear, caught in a leafless brake,
Breathless with wonder and the tears half-dried
Upon her rosy cheek; summer shall come
And waste his passion like a prodigal
Right royally; and autumn spend her gold
Free-handed as a harlot; men to know,
Women to love are waiting everywhere.'

ROMANCE

The Merchantman

The Markethaunters

The Markethaunters : Now, while our money is pip-
    ing hot
From the mint of our toil that coins the sheaves,
Merchantman, merchantman, what have you got
    In your tabernacle hung with leaves ?
        What have you got ?
        The sun rides high;
        Our money is hot;
        We must buy, buy, buy!

The Merchantman : I come from the elfin king's
    demesne
With chrysolite, hyacinth, tourmaline;
I have emeralds here of living green;
    I have rubies, each like a cup of wine;
And diamonds, diamonds that never have been
    Outshone by eyes the most divine!

The Markethaunters: Jewellery ?—Baubles; bad for
    the soul;
  Desire of the heart and lust of the eye!

Diamonds, indeed!   We wanted coal.
  What else do you sell ?   Come, sound your cry'
      Our money is hot;
        The night draws nigh;
      What have you got
        That we want to buy ?

The Merchantman: I have here enshrined the soul of
    the rose
  Exhaled in the land of the daystar's birth;
I have casks whose golden staves enclose
  Eternal youth, eternal mirth;
And cordials that bring repose,
  And the tranquil night, and the end of the earth.

The Markethaunters : Rapture of wine ? But it never
    pays:
We must keep our common-sense alert.
Raisins are healthier, medicine says—
  Raisins and almonds for dessert.
      But we want to buy;
        For our money is hot,
      And age draws nigh:
        What else have you got?

The Merchantman: I have lamps that gild the lustre
        of noon;
   Shadowy arrows that pierce the brain;
Dulcimers strung with beams of the moon;
   Psalteries fashioned of pleasure and pain;
A song and a sword and a haunting tune
   That may never be offered the world again.

The Markethaunters: Dulcimers! psalteries! Whom
        do you mock?
   Arrows and songs?   We have axes to grind!
Shut up your booth and your mouldering stock,
   For we never shall deal.—Come away; let us find
            What the others have got
               We must buy, buy, buy;
            For our money is hot,
               And death draws nigh.

INSOMNIA

HE wakened quivering on a golden rack
    Inlaid with gems: no sign of change, no fear
    Or hope of death came near;
Only the empty ether hovered black
    About him stretched upon his living bier,
Of old by Merlin's Master deftly wrought:
    Two Seraphim of Gabriel's helpful race
    In that far nook of space
With iron levers wrenched and held him taut.

The Seraph at his head was Agony;
    Delight, more terrible, stood at his feet:
    Their sixfold pinions beat
The darkness, or were spread immovably
    Poising the rack, whose jewelled fabric meet
To strain a god, did fitfully unmask
    With olive light of chrysoprases dim
    The smiling Seraphim
Implacably intent upon their task.

SERENADE

(1250 A.D.)

W ITH stars, with trailing galaxies,
  Like a white-rose bower in bloom,
Darkness garlands the vaulted skies,
  Day's ethereal tomb;
A whisper without from the briny west
  Thrills and sweetens the gloom;
Within, Miranda seeks her rest
  High in her turret-room.

Armies upon her walls encamp
  In silk and silver thread;
Chased and fretted, her silver lamp
  Dimly lights her bed;
And now the silken screen is drawn,
  The velvet coverlet spread;
And the pillow of down and snowy lawn
  Mantles about her head.

With violet-scented rain
  Sprinkle the rushy floor;
Let the tapestry hide the tinted pane,
  And cover the chamber door;
But leave a glimmering beam,

Miranda belamour,
To touch and gild my waking dream,
For I am your troubadour.

I sound my throbbing lyre,
And sing to myself below;|
Her damsel sits beside the fire
Crooning a song I know;
The tapestry shakes on the wall,
The shadows hurry and go,
The silent flames leap up and fall,
And the muttering birch-logs glow.

Deep and sweet she sleeps,
Because of her love for me;
And deep and sweet the peace that keeps
My happy heart in fee!
Peace on the heights, in the deeps,
Peace over hill and lea,
Peace through the star-lit steeps,
Peace on the starlit sea,
Because a simple maiden sleeps
Dreaming a dream of me!

THE LAST ROSE

' Oh, which is the last rose ? '
A blossom of no name.
At midnight the snow came;
At daybreak a vast rose,
In darkness unfurled,
O'er-petaled the world.

Its odourless pallor,
Blossomed forlorn,
Till radiant valour
Established the morn—
Till the night
Was undone
In her fight
With the sun.

The brave orb in state rose
And crimson he shone first;
While from the high vine
Of heaven the dawn burst,
Staining the great rose
From sky-line to sky-line.

The red rose of morn
A white rose at noon turned;
But at sunset reborn,
All red again soon burned.
Then the pale rose of noonday
Re-bloomed in the night,
And spectrally white
In the light
Of the moon lay.

But the vast rose
Was scentless,
And this is the reason·
When the blast rose
Relentless,
And brought in due season
The snow-rose, the last rose
Congealed in its breath,
There came with it treason;
The traitor was Death.

In lee-valleys crowded,
The sheep and the birds
Were frozen and shrouded
In flights and in herds.
In highways
And byways
The young and the old

Were tortured and maddened
And killed by the cold.
But many were gladdened
By the beautiful last rose,
The blossom of no name
That came when the snow came,
In darkness unfurled—
The wonderful vast rose
That filled all the world.

SONG OF A TRAIN

A MONSTER taught
To come to hand
Amain,
As swift as thought
Across the land
The train.

The song it sings
Has an iron sound;
Its iron wings
Like wheels go round.

Crash under bridges,
Flash over ridges,
And vault the downs;
The road is straight—
Nor stile, nor gate;
For milestones—towns!

Voluminous, vanishing, white,
The steam plume trails;
Parallel streaks of light,
The polished rails.

Oh, who can follow?
The little swallow,
The trout of the sky:
But the sun
Is outrun,
And Time passed by.

O'er bosky dens,
By marsh and mead,
Forest and fens
Embodied speed
Is clanked and hurled;
O'er rivers and runnels;
And into the earth
And out again
In death and birth
That know no pain,
For the whole round world
Is a warren of railway tunnels.

Hark! hark! hark!
It screams and cleaves the dark;
And the subterranean night
Is gilt with smoky light.
Then out again apace
It runs its thundering race,
The monster taught
To come to hand

Amain,
That swift as thought
Speeds through the land
The train.

A LOAFER

I HANG about the streets all day,
  At night I hang about;
I sleep a little when I may,
  But rise betimes the morning's scout;
For through the year I always hear
  Afar, aloft, a ghostly shout.

My clothes are worn to threads and loops;
  My skin shows here and there;
About my face like seaweed droops
  My tangled beard, my tangled hair;
From cavernous and shaggy brows
  My stony eyes untroubled stare.

I move from eastern wretchedness
  Through Fleet Street and the Strand;
And as the pleasant people press
  I touch them softly with my hand,
Perhaps to know that still I go
  Alive about a living land.

For, far in front the clouds are riven;
  I heard the ghostly cry,

As if a still voice fell from heaven
  To where sea-whelmed the drowned folks lie
In sepulchres no tempest stirs
  And only eyeless things pass by.

In Piccadilly spirits pass:
  Oh, eyes and cheeks that glow!
Oh, strength and comeliness!   Alas,
  The lustrous health is earth I know
From shrinking eyes that recognise
  No brother in my rags and woe.

I know no handicraft, no art,
  But I have conquered fate;
For I have chosen the better part,
  And neither hope, nor fear, nor hate.
With placid breath on pain and death,
  My certain alms, alone I wait.

And daily, nightly comes the call,
  The pale, unechoing note,
The faint 'Aha!' sent from the wall
  Of heaven, but from no ruddy throat
Of human breed or seraph's seed,
  A phantom voice that cries by rote.

MATINEE

From the night-haunt where vapours crowd
　　The airy outskirts of the earth
A winding caravan of cloud
　　Rose when the morning's punctual hearth
Began to charm the winds and skies
With odours fresh and golden dyes.

It made a conquest of the sun,
　　And tied his beams; but, in the game
Of hoodman-blind, the rack, outdone,
　　Beheld the brilliant captive claim
Forfeit on forfeit, as he pressed
The mountains to his burning breast.

Above the path by vapours trod
　　A ringing causey seemed to be,
Whereby the orient, silver-shod,
　　Rode out across the Atlantic sea,
An embassy of valour sent
Under the echoing firmament.

But while the hearkener divined
　　A clanging cavalcade on high,

This rush and trample of the wind
   Arose among the tree-tops nigh,
For mystery is the craft profound,
The sign, and ancient trade of sound.

An unseen roadman breaking flint,
   If echo and the winds conspire
To dedicate his morning's stint,
   May beat a tune out, dew and fire
So wrought that heaven might lend an ear,
And Ariel hush his harp to hear.

HOLIDAY AT HAMPTON COURT

SCALES of pearly cloud inlay
  North and south the turquoise sky,
While the diamond lamp of day
  Quenchless burns, and time on high
A moment halts upon his way
  Bidding noon again good-bye.

Gaffers, gammers, huzzies, louts,
  Couples, gangs, and families
Sprawling, shake, with Babel-shouts
  Bluff King Hal's funereal trees;
And eddying groups of stare-abouts
  Quiz the sandstone Hercules.

When their tongues and tempers tire,
  Harry and his little lot
Condescendingly admire
  Lozenge-bed and crescent-plot,
Aglow with links of azure fire,
  Pansy and forget-me-not.

Where the emerald shadows rest
  In the lofty woodland aisle,

Chaffing lovers quaintly dressed
    Chase and double many a mile,
Indifferent exiles in the west
    Making love in cockney style.

Now the echoing palace fills;
    Men and women, girls and boys
Trample past the swords and frills,
    Kings and Queens and trulls and toys;
Or listening loll on window-sills,
    Happy amateurs of noise!

That for pictured rooms of state!
    Out they hurry, wench and knave,
Where beyond the palace-gate
    Dusty legions swarm and rave,
With laughter, shriek, inane debate,
    Kentish fire and comic stave.

Voices from the river call;
    Organs hammer tune on tune;
Larks triumphant over all
    Herald twilight coming soon,
For as the sun begins to fall
    Near the zenith gleams the moon.

THIRTY BOB A WEEK

I COULDN'T touch a stop and turn a screw,
  And set the blooming world a-work for me,
Like such as cut their teeth—I hope, like you—
  On the handle of a skeleton gold key;
I cut mine on a leek, which I eat it every week:
  I'm a clerk at thirty bob as you can see.

But I don't allow it's luck and all a toss;
  There's no such thing as being starred and crossed;
It's just the power of some to be a boss,
  And the bally power of others to be bossed:
I face the music, sir; you bet I ain't a cur;
  Strike me lucky if I don't believe I'm lost!

For like a mole I journey in the dark,
  A-travelling along the underground
From my Pillar'd Halls and broad Suburbean Park,
  To come the daily dull official round;
And home again at night with my pipe all alight,
  A-scheming how to count ten bob a pound.

And it's often very cold and very wet,
  And my missis stitches towels for a hunks;

And the Pillar'd Halls is half of it to let—
　　Three rooms about the size of travelling trunks.
And we cough, my wife and I, to dislocate a sigh,
　　When the noisy little kids are in their bunks.

But you never hear her do a growl or whine,
　　For she's made of flint and roses, very odd;
And I've got to cut my meaning rather fine,
　　Or I'd blubber, for I'm made of greens and sod:
So p'r'aps we are in Hell for all that I can tell,
　　And lost and damn'd and served up hot to God.

I ain't blaspheming, Mr. Silver-tongue;
　　I'm saying things a bit beyond your art:
Of all the rummy starts you ever sprung,
　　Thirty bob a week's the rummiest start!
With your science and your books and your the'ries
　　　　about spooks,
　　Did you ever hear of looking in your heart?

I didn't mean your pocket, Mr., no:
　　I mean that having children and a wife,
With thirty bob on which to come and go,
　　Isn't dancing to the tabor and the fife:
When it doesn't make you drink, by Heaven! it makes
　　　　you think,
　　And notice curious items about life.

I step into my heart and there I meet
   A god-almighty devil singing small,
Who would like to shout and whistle in the street,
   And squelch the passers flat against the wall;
If the whole world was a cake he had the power to take,
   He would take it, ask for more, and eat them all.

And I meet a sort of simpleton beside,
   The kind that life is always giving beans;
With thirty bob a week to keep a bride
   He fell in love and married in his teens:
At thirty bob he stuck; but he knows it isn't luck·
   He knows the seas are deeper than tureens.

And the god-almighty devil and the fool
   That meet me in the High Street on the strike,
When I walk about my heart a-gathering wool,
   Are my good and evil angels if you like.
And both of them together in every kind of weather
   Ride me like a double-seated bike.

That's rough a bit and needs its meaning curled.
   But I have a high old hot un in my mind—
A most engrugious notion of the world,
   That leaves your lightning 'rithmetic behind:
I give it at a glance when I say ' There ain't no chance,
   Nor nothing of the lucky-lottery kind.'

And it's this way that I make it out to be·
　　No fathers, mothers, countries, climates—none;
Not Adam was responsible for me,
　　Nor society, nor systems, nary one·
A little sleeping seed, I woke—I did, indeed—
　　A million years before the blooming sun.

I woke because I thought the time had come;
　　Beyond my will there was no other cause;
And everywhere I found myself at home,
　　Because I chose to be the thing I was ; '
And in whatever shape of mollusc or of ape
　　I always went according to the laws.

I was the love that chose my mother out;
　　I joined two lives and from the union burst;
My weakness and my strength without a doubt
　　Are mine alone for ever from the first:
It's just the very same with a difference in the name
　　As ' Thy will be done.'　You say it if you durst!

They say it daily up and down the land
　　As easy as you take a drink, it's true;
But the difficultest go to understand,
　　And the difficultest job a man can do,
Is to come it brave and meek with thirty bob a week,
　　And feel that that's the proper thing for you.

It's a naked child against a hungry wolf;
 It's playing bowls upon a splitting wreck;
It's walking on a string across a gulf
 With millstones fore-and-aft about your neck;
But the thing is daily done by many and many a one·
 And we fall, face forward, fighting, on the deck.

THE OUTCAST

Soul, be your own
  Pleasance and mart,
A land unknown,
  A state apart.

Scowl, and be rude
  Should love entice;
Call gratitude
  The costliest vice.

Deride the ill
  By fortune sent;
Be scornful still
  If foes repent.

When curse and stone
  Are hissed and hurled,
Aloof, alone
  Disdain the world.

Soul, disregard
  The bad, the good;
Be haughty, hard,
  Misunderstood.

Be neutral; spare
　　No humblest lie,
And overbear
　　Authority.

Laugh wisdom down;
　　Abandon fate;
Shame the renown
　　Of all the great.

Dethrone the past;
　　Deed, vision—naught
Avails at last
　　Save your own thought.

Though on all hands
　　The powers unsheathe
Their lightning-brands
　　And from beneath,

And from above
　　One curse be hurled
With scorn, with love
　　Affront the world,

THE PIONEER

WHY, he never can tell;
  But, without a doubt,
He knows very well
  He must trample out
Through forest and fell
  The world about
A way for himself,
A way for himself.

By sun and star,
  Forlorn and lank,
O'er cliff and scar,
  O'er bog and bank,
He hears afar
  The expresses clank,
' You'll never get there,
You'll never get there!'

His bones and bread
  Poor Turlygod
From his wallet spread
  On the grass-green sod,
And stared and said

H

With a mow and a nod,
‘ Whither away, sir,
Whither away ? ’

‘ I’m going alone,
   Though Hell forfend,
By a way of my own
   To the bitter end.’
He gnawed a bone
   And snarled, ‘ My friend,
You’ll soon get there,
You’ll soon get there.’

But whether or no,
   The world is round;
And he still must go
   Through depths profound,
O’er heights of snow,
   On virgin ground
To find a grave,
To find a grave.

For he knows very well
   He must trample out
Through Heaven and Hell,
   With never a doubt,
A way of his own
   The world about.

THE HERO

My thought sublimes
  A common deed;
In evil times
  In utmost need,
My spirit climbs
  Where dragons breed.

Nor will I trip
  Even at the hiss
On the drawn lip
  Of the abyss:
My footsteps grip
  The precipice.

Applause and blame
  Let prophets share:
My secret aim
  The deed I dare,
My own acclaim
  Comprise my care.

Above the laws,
   Against the light
That overawes
   The world I fight
And win. because
   I have the might.

THE ORDEAL

BETWEEN the Golden City and the sea
A damasked meadow lay, the saffron beach
And silver loops of surge dissevering
The violet water from the grass-green land.

While yet the morning sun swung low in heaven,
A crystal censer in a turquoise dome,
Emanuel meted justice in the gate,
Emanuel of the Golden City King.
To him there came Sir Hilary; his wife,
The comely Bertha; after them their sons
And daughters grieving. Godfrey also came,
Knight-errant of the Phœnix; from that quest
Lately returned: guarded he was and bound.

'Justice, my lord and king!' cried Hilary,
With passion hoarse, and wanner than a flame
That flickers in the sun. 'I saw them kiss:
I saw her from her bosom take a ring
And place it warm upon his finger. Here'—
He gave the King the ring—'an old worn hoop
Of pale alloy, but clasping, doubt it not,
A horde of sweet and shameful memories

More dear to them than mines of virgin gold.
Justice, my lord and king!'

          'Whom do you charge?'

'Sir Godfrey and my wife.   I saw them kiss;
I saw her tearfully assign the ring
Warm from her bosom to his lustful hand.
For him the gallows and for her the stake!'

'But if you saw this done, Sir Hilary,
Why is her lover here alive to-day?'

'I ran upon him in the garden-close
When I espied them; but he beat me back.
Hearing the clash of steel my folk rushed forth
And fettered him.   Vengeance miscarrying thus,
Before the world the law shall have its way.
The age is dissolute; the hearts of men
Know every sin by rote; their starveling souls
Are blind and lame: I publish my disgrace
To warn the world.   This woman is my wife;
These well-grown youths; these budding damsels—
      look . . .
I scarce can say the words   look you, my
     liege,
These are our children: treasure, you would say,
To fill a woman's heart?   Oh no!   He there,

That lecher, is her lover, gray and gaunt.
If she be burned before her children's eyes,
The wanton blood they have from her, refined
By fire, in her fierce torment drained and seared,
May leave them humble-hearted and afraid
Even of the lawful kiss of married love.
Justice, my lord, upon the shameful pair!'

'Do they admit the charge?   What do you say,
Sir Godfrey?   Bertha, answer.'

                              'All my life,'
The lady said, looking upon the ground:
Because when she looked up her stricken eyes
Turned to her children, sorrowing by her side;
And her true heart when most she needed strength
Began to break: wherefore upon the ground
She cast her gaze and answered, 'All my life
I have been faithful to my husband's bed.'

'And I,' said Godfrey, 'never did him wrong.'

Knight-errant of the Phœnix, fancy-charmed
At fifty still, but as inept to lie
As tongueless men to sing, even furtive minds
A grudging credence paid him: jealousy
That calls the moon a leper, and will swear
There never was a maid of sweet sixteen,

Only the heart's attorney, jealousy,
Had any countenance to doubt his word.

'He lies,' cried Hilary, 'as the lovers' code
Requires.'

'The ring, the keepsake?' said the King:
'Did you receive it with a kiss from her?'

'I kissed her, and she gave me back the ring.'

'Oh! she returned the ring!' cried Hilary.
'A stale, old shame! I might have guessed as much.
The happiest of men I judged myself.
My wife, so delicate, so meek, so chaste,
A rare obedience gave; but unperfumed,
Unlit by passion: so she seemed, and so
To me she was, because her false blood burned
In the dark-lantern of a lawless love.
Where did he hunt the Phœnix? Ask him that.
How often has he, wandering secretly,
Discovered in my arbours, here at home,
Or on my pillows, Araby the Blest?'

'Nay,' said the King; 'have patience, Hilary.
Let Godfrey plead; she after him shall tell
Her own romance. Lead her aside meanwhile.'

'Content,' said Hilary.

                And it was done.
Her children gathered round her as she went,
Worship and sorrow fighting in their looks.
The youngest, eager to be near her, trod
Upon her skirt, making her halt.   Abashed
He shrank behind the others; but she turned,
And, seeing him distressed, held out her hand,
Moving her fingers as she used to do
Winningly when her children first could walk.
She sent him also so humane a smile,
So sweet, so patient, that his ruddy cheek
Grew pale as hers; and, suffering more than she,
Because he hardly knew—and yet he knew—
The naked meaning of his father's charge,
He cried aloud, and, throttled by his sobs,
Sank to the ground: the mounting tide of life
Had but begun to press upon his heart
With murmured news of mystery unveiled;
And all his fancy innocently clung
About his mother—he, her latest born;
And she, his earliest sweetheart.

                Silently,
Before another could, she reached her son,
And lifted him and bore him in her arms.
Dismayed to find himself a babe again,
He pushed her from him, straining towards the
     ground.

'Be still!' she said,   'This is a thing to do!
Something to do!' and crushed him to her breast.

East of the city wall a virgin wood
Discovered twilight gleams of emerald
In depths of leafy darkness treasured up.
Upon its verge a grove of hawthorn hung,
The friendly tree—and Nature's favourite:
For now that all its own unhoarded bloom
Was withered, and its incense sacrificed,
The honeysuckle lit the matted boughs
With cressets burning odour, and the briar
Enwreathed and overhung them lovingly,
Its pallid rose like elfin faces sweet
Peering from out the swart-green thicket-side.

Thither they led dame Bertha.   In the shade
She sat: her son, still as a nursling now,
With solemn eyes where stately dreams reside,
Lay in her arms and watched her ashen lips.
The brilliant blackbirds, sauntering through the brake,
Doled out indifferently their golden notes,
Or sprinkled magic phrases, summer showers
Of jewelled rain, the while Sir Godfrey's voice
Re-echoed faintly from the City gate.
Then Bertha, all benumbed with misery,
Caressed her son, and, swaying to and fro,
In troubled whispers told a fairy tale

Of how a lady, deeply wronged, became
The happiest princess in the world at last.
Her other children, kneeling by her side,
Powerless to comfort, worshipped her and wept.

Sir Godfrey, standing bound before the King,
Spoke thus: ' My cognizance has wrought my fate:
A Phœnix burning in his nest; the scroll,
Viget in cinere virtus.   In my youth
I swore to find the Phœnix, being scorned
By many who averred that no such fowl
Inhabited the earth.   And here, my lord,
Before I answer Hilary's reproach,
I beg all men to know the Phœnix lives;
For I have seen him fly across the Nile,
Beating the air with gold and purple plumes,
Towards Yemen, where he reigns: this was last year,
The thirtieth of my quest.'

                     ' Sir,' said the King:
' I marvel at your patience.   Thirty years!'
' Patience ?   I know it not!   Embarked, I swore
That thirty weeks, and sorely grudged the time,
Should see the Phœnix caught and caged; myself,
Renowned throughout the world, and fixed in fame
With Lancelot and Roland.   Youth and hope
Spare none of us—Syren and Circe linked
In one divine betrayal of the world!

Even while the Golden City towered behind
And bathed its glittering shadow in the deep
The Berber galleys swooped: captivity
Her twisted talons settled in my flesh
To tire on body and soul with dripping beak
For thrice the time I vowed.   That was the dawn!
Also in Hadramaut, five savage years
Of lash and shackle, scornful destiny
Awarded me.   Tenacious death, in shapes
Of thraldom, pestilence, contention, thirst,
Shipwreck and famine, flame and blind despair,
Remained my mate by day, my watch by night.
Yet, and although I still am buffeted
By every busy wind and stroke of chance:
Deceived, disgraced, contemptuously foiled
By oracles, by wantonness of fools,
And by the sleepless masked malignity
That men pursue the soul of man withal,
I am neither taught nor tamed.   Intolerance
Of mundane things—of utter sanctity
As of indulged desire—shines in the stars,
And in the icy menace of the moon.
From them my fire is kindled, keenest flame
Of passion; for I look not to be praised
Here in the courts of Kings and homes of men;
Nor happily hereafter to usurp
A blissful throne of that imagined world
By terror-stricken envy reared in air

For the immortal solace and reward
Of humbleness and chastity, the true
Accomplices, the virtuous other selves
Of mediocrity and impotence.
But I desire to follow out this quest:
Achieved or unachieved it is my own:
Even if the glorious creature were no more   .
A foolish word!   I have seen him, as I said:
From Heliopolis he took his flight
Towards Yemen, like a rainbow laced with gems.
Whether I find him, or am overthrown
Pursuing him, the world shall never know:
My purpose is sufficient for my soul.
Farewell at once.   I must be gone—again
To feel my heart leap at the sudden foe,
The lonely battle in the wilderness;
To come at night under the desert moon
On pillars, ghostly porches, temples, towers
Silent for centuries; to see at dawn
The shadow of the Arab on the sand.'

Sir Godfrey bowed and strode a pace away;
Then stopped like one enchanted, wondering
What spell o'ermastered him.   When from his dream
He woke, and felt his pinioned arms, a blush
Shone on his tawny cheek and untanned brow.
He muttered something quickly; stumbled—stood,
Staring before him.

                              ' Mediocrity
And impotence!' cried Hilary.   ' The phrase,
The very motto lechery inscribes
Beneath the cuckold's sign armorial,
Crested dilemma, honour's hatchment, horns.
This Phœnix-hunt, this magpie-tale of his
Allures no sober judgment from the nest
He fouled!   Incredible effrontery!'
' Not in my thought, Sir Hilary,' said the King.
' I cannot press a finger on the wrist
Of treason, and declare ' This blood is false ';
Nor is there a divining-rod for kings
To tell the hearts of gold; but I dare stake
My Crown against an apple that the man
Is honest: he forgot the charge preferred
Against him.—Answer me: How came you, sir,
To be discovered with Sir Hilary's wife ? '

' Oh, very simply!' said Sir Godfrey.

                                   ' Ay!'
Groaned Hilary in his beard; ' simply enough!'
' When I at last beheld the Phœnix, watched
His dazzling flight stream through the eastern air,
The sun fell down behind me, and my heart
Beset me in the darkness.   Overpowered
By deep desire to repossess a ring
That was my mother's . . . Many men, my lord,

Of hardihood sufficient have been known
To hold the memories of their mothers dear
I told myself that having seen once more
The Golden City, wandered through its streets
Of cheerful folk, and by the windy wharfs
Where silent shipmen hang about, and stir
The hearts of passers strangely, never more
Should any thought withdraw me from my quest.
As for the ring, I knew not Hilary's wife
Possessed it; but I knew that Bertha did.
It happened thus: At twenty years, alone
And penniless, house, trinkets—all I sold
To furnish fame with wings; and straightway shipped
For Egypt and the Phœnix.   Ere we sailed
I saw this Bertha wistfully approach,
And ran to her, for we were pleasant friends—
Sweethearts, perhaps.   Younger than I she was,
And like a palm-tree tall and lithe.   I think
Until that day I had not said one word
Of love; but in the morning, half in jest,
Shamefast I whispered, bidding her good-bye,
'And will you marry me when I come back?'
Her blood dyed all her face and neck deep red:
She leaned aside and gazed askance with looks
As wide as day; then fronted me.   Her sighs
Beat from her open mouth hot on my face
Like scented winds that blow in Hadramaut.
She trembled, sobbed, and while I wondered fled—

In anger or in love I could not tell.'
'Ay, ay!' went Hilary, with the dog-like leer
Of one whose ribs are grilled by torturers.

'But when she sought me out upon the ship,
And silently embraced me meeting her,
I knew, I surely knew that it was love.
She knotted in my scarf a silken purse,
And said, 'A keepsake.   Give me something, sir.'
The ring, my lord, was all I had to give.
I would have pawned, as I have spent, my soul
To serve my purpose: that metallic lie,
My mother's talisman—its paltriness
As merchandise and unappraisable
Romance preserved it.   Often I had watched
My mother turn and turn it lost in thought;
And watching I divined its history.
With hoarded pence, my father, straitly kept,
Had bought it for her on a festival
When they were children: love began with them
In April: and she showed me—for I asked
If I divined aright—half-hidden zones
Engraved as with her ripening the ring
On divers fingers had reposed in turn.
Quickly at Bertha's vehement desire
I offered the remembrance I had kept.
She stretched her hand—a fragrant lily hand,
And slipped a petal through the pinchbeck hoop;

Then clad me in her glance and stole away.
Now that I think, I never have beheld
In any other face or other eyes
Of man or woman, or hero in my dreams,
So great a passion, so profound a hope.'

' Ha! ' cried the King.   ' Regret has found you out ?'

' Oh no, my lord!   My spirit stands aloof
In judgment of the past.   The Moorish whips
Cut from my fancy Bertha's image, pale
Even at the start.   Scarcely, until I longed
To have my mother's ring, did any thought
Of Bertha's love offend me in my quest.
After delays—the lackeys circumstance
Provides abundantly for all my schemes—
I reached the Golden City.   Hilary's wife,
They told me, was the Bertha I had known.
I found her house, and seeing her without—
It could be no one else; indeed I seemed
To catch her walk again—I went to her,
Withdrawn among a grove of cypresses,
And asked her headlong for my mother's ring.
She gave it me, as Hilary says, and looked,
Poor soul, so sad, that pity wrung my heart.
I kissed her brow: down fell the silvery tears,
And thrice she tried to speak: but Hilary came
And made this ugly rent in our adieus.

'This is the truth,' said King Emanuel.

'Lies!   Subtle lies!' the husband hissed. 'Hear her!
The trap he sets himself.   If her account
Accord with his, chance deals in mirac'es.'

Said Godfrey then, ' My lord, I kissed his wife,
And therefore overlook the littleness
Of his attack; but now that he has heard
The truth, and still denies my honesty,
I claim the combat.'

                    ' And the claim is just,'
Emanuel said.   ' I stand for God; but step
Aside, well-pleased that He should arbitrate
Immediately.   So, let the lists be set.'

' But Bertha's story ?' stammered Hilary.

' Sir,' said the King.   ' The combat shall decide
Whether your wife requires to plead or no.'

' Well—very well!' said Hilary.   ' I am old;
My joints are stiff; my sinews slack; my sight
Begins to fail; 'tis ebbtide in my blood:
He like a lion from the desert comes
Supple and strong with questing up and down.
Behold an opportunity for God—
Which He will profit by!'

‘I doubt it not,’
The King said meaningly.

But Godfrey said,
‘What prate is this ? I am the better man,
And Hilary shall fall before my lance.’

At noon the lists were set. About the earth,
Whose sea-enamelled disk resplendent wheeled
Among the hidden stars, deep-bosomed clouds,
Horizon-haunting, towered and stooped; the sun
Poured from his quenchless urn, high-held in heaven,
A silent cataract of light, whereto
The mounting larks with sinewy wings and throats
Of tempered gold harnessed a voice inspired.
But in the shining City the tilt-yard hummed
With the inhuman gossip of the world—
The lickerish crowd agape to dip their mouths
In purple-streaming agony, distrained
From hearts mature for torture, newly plucked
And cast into the press.

Emanuel,
When as the sullen-sounding bell had rung
The heavy peal of noon, gave forth the word.
Straightway the trumpets rang, and every look
Towards Bertha veered at once. The petulant throng
Again and yet again, with puckered brows

And hands aslant against the naked light,
Had prowled and peered, and launched surmises wide
Of her repose and countenance serene—
Inscrutable to eyes of cavillers;
But now the winepress flowed, the bout began
With winks and elbowings and nimble nods.
For at the trumpets' call a scarlet sign
Flashed up on Bertha's face; and from the post
Where opposite the King she stood alone,
Patient and proud, a smile of utter peace,
A shaft of glory on her children fell;
And they, disburdened, stretched their hands and
        laughed:
Since God Himself had hung His balance out,
Already they could hear the host of Heaven,
With psalteries and far-resounding songs,
Acclaim their mother's starry chastity,
And laud the righteous Judge of all the earth.

A second time the trumpets rang—a cry
Implacable with shrieking echoes winged;
Then silence like a heavy dew came down.
Before a breath could move the stagnant air,
And while the pennoned lances of the twain—
Godfrey and Hilary in arms of proof—
Upon the summons in the sockets couched
Still quivered pausing, overthwart the lists
A vagrant bee twanged like an airy lyre

Of one rich-hearted chord.   Swift underneath
The honey-laden track the gleaming hoofs
Of either spur-wrung charger gripped the ground,
Flung forth and spanned the course with fluent speed
Of thudding leaps entwined.   Together hurled
In uncontrolled assault—each rivet wrenched,
Each nerve and artery of horse and man
Shot through with scalding flame—helm-smitten, both
Hung overborne and toppling urgently,
Till Hilary in his stirrups rose and screamed,
Startling his mastered steed, ' Go down to Hell '—
Astounded at his triumph and meanly glad
That Godfrey should have fallen pierced through the
            brain
By his haphazard, his unworthy lance,
' Go down to Hell, and cook your Phœnix there! '

The instant murmur of the tossing crowd
Sprang to a roar; and like a home-sick wretch
Delivered from the storm whose gliding hull
Founders upon the welcome harbour-bar,
The voice of malice thrust into her ears
Even as the din and hubbub of the sea
Deafens the drowning outcast, Bertha fell
Wrecked in the very haven of her hope.

Her children, led by him whom she had nursed
To cheat the time beneath the hawthorn-shade,

Tongue-tied with grief and dazzled by their tears,
But bright instinctive creatures in the speed
And promptness of their act, maidens and youths,
O'er skipped the barrier.   Bertha then, sustained
By hands of love that trembled and were strong,
Arose, and midmost of her brood at bay
Confronted the eclipse of her renown.

His latticed vizor raised, Sir Hilary cried
Above the dwindled clamour, 'Heaven has judged,
Oh King Emanuel!   Bid her now confess!'

'I bid her speak.   Speak, Bertha,' said the King,
Heart-struck and pale, but waiting yet on God;
While all the quidnuncs inly hugged themselves,
And market-haunters chafed their sweaty palms,
For now, indeed, the winepress overflowed.

Heading her cygnets, Bertha paced the lists
Towards the throne, a stately sufferer.
Her curtsy not forgotten, and her glance
Sweeping the gazers till it lit and hung
Upon the watchful King; in either hand
A child's close-clasped; and in her bosom pent
A tide of tears, she stood till silence reigned,
Then lifted up a sick and shuddering voice.

But Hilary broke out, 'What need, my lord?

The judgment has been given : the sentence now
Is all that should be said.'

               ' Your best and worst
Is said and done!' the King declared. ' What should
And should not be, who dare assume ?   God's mind
Is not apparent yet.   Your wife shall speak.'

' Now, is this just ? ' said Hilary.

             ' Just ? ' she cried.
' My children at my skirt, before the world,
My zealous husband and the King and God,
I wish to speak!'   Intolerant at last,
Her mouth distorted and her eyes on fire,
She threw her piercing challenge out: ' My love
Was never Hilary's!'   That said, she paused,
The mistress of her audience.   Slowly then
She bent her gaze on Godfrey's mail-clad corpse:
Through the crushed beaver—the floodgate of his life—
A crimson current sluiced his helm, and stained
With ruddy umber a sodden patch of sand.
But steadfastly she looked and proudly spake:
' I loved the dead man there.   O King, O God '—
Now to the earthly throne and now to heaven—
' His was the face and form adored the most
By noble maidens, grave and ardent: his
The highest heart, the freest soul of all

The aspirants of the City in the days
When love laid claim to us who now are old.
In dreams and potent melancholy steeped
I felt the subtle essence, the desire,
  The pure, unmingled virtue of my life
Yield up itself, a suppliant passion, bound
To minister to his, or waste away
The impatient captive of his memory.
He loved me as a young man loves who knows
By hearsay only of the deeds of love—
As virgins love he loved me; but without
The overwhelming anguish I endured,
I being a woman.   When at last he spoke
It was not till the luckless day he sailed
On his adventure: 'Would I marry him
When he came back?'   My heart took fire: it
          seemed
To melt and flow: speech failed me and I fled.
But in the evening, when the land-breeze blew,
Breathless I hurried through the murmuring streets
Refreshed with scent of meadow-hay new-reaped
Behind the Golden City.   He saw me come
Staring along the quay; he leapt ashore;
He kissed me: but the ropes were casting off;
The ripple beat and chid his tardy barque.
I twisted in his dress a silken purse
With twenty golden ducats of my own;
He on my finger thrust that piteous ring:

And straight the sundering ocean lay between,
All in the springtime thirty years ago.'

'A perfect tale,' cried Hilary.   'A plot
Nicely prepared!'

                 'I have not done,' she said.
'Love like a dragon breathing smoke and armed
In jewelled scales withdrew me to the den
Of starless night his burning orbs illume.
Whene'er I struggled in that dreadful hold,
Where only long-drawn sighs are heard and groans
Unpitied ever, adamantine fangs
Were mortised in my heart.   So clutched and torn,
Year after year I waited on my knight,
My lover, to deliver me from love.
But madness came instead and death stood near:
These the abounding vigour of my race,
And youth, long-suffering, quickly overpowered.
Forthwith to blight my new-blown summer-time
The vision of my hero dawned once more,
And at my chamber-window in the night
I saw the jewelled dragon vigilant.
Then was it that I turned to thee, O God
Who madest me!   'Thy handmaid, Lord,' I said;
'Pity Thy handmaid!   Him whom I adore
On earth the most—in Thine own image shaped
More excellently than all men beside—

Has wandered over sea: no message comes,
No token; none report him; he is lost—
Is dead to me, for I am more than thought.
Must I descend into the dust again
And of my body see no fruit at all ?
O God, the heaped-up treasure of delight
Garnered by Thee within me, may no man
Unlock it but the loved one ?   Must I clasp
No child of my own womb if he be dead
Or come not back to me ?   O God, dear God.,
I did not make myself : Thy strong desire
Consumes me   Help me ! help me !'—On the night
I wrestled thus in prayer, divine content
Descended tranquilly and overbrimmed
My famished heart; the lurking dragon whirled
His jewelled mail away, his blood-stained fangs·
And at my chamber-window watching me,
And beckoning, and waiting to be born,
The seraph faces of my children pressed.
In widow's weeds I tarried one year more,
Then chose Sir Hilary from out my throng
Of honourable blandishers to be
The father of my children—stately then
And tall, a personable gentleman
Some ten years older than myself : sedate
He seemed and wise—his fame without a flaw.
I told him though I had no love to give
I should be proud to be his faithful wife

And bosom-friend. That pleased him best, he said—
Lying, because he strove to make of me
An instrument of pleasure for himself;
But like Zenobia, noblest of her sex,
I kept my babes unsullied. Look at them!'

She stepped behind her children, seven in all—
Four lustrous youths, three maidens lovelier
Than seraphs hallowed visionaries see.
'These are my witnesses.' Emanuel
Bent towards them, blessing them. Sir Hilary,
Hell glimmering in his visage, gnawed his tongue,
And let his beaver down.

                    'My Bertha here'—
Taking her eldest daughter by the hand—
'Sleepless all night, this morning to my room
Came blushing with the dawn. Beside me couched,
She told the tale of passion Sigismund
Beneath the evening star had told to her,
And in my arms fell peacefully asleep.'

At once a page attendant on the King
Vaulted the barrier, and took his post
Beside the younger Bertha, overjoyed
To find his suit accepted, and of right
Claiming a share in what should now befall
His lady's house. The elder Bertha smiled

A welcome, tender of any happiness
Even in her misery; then made an end.

' My daughter's passion wakened from the grave
The memory of the wonder-working stir
And daybreak of my womanhood.   I stole
The ring—to me it seemed indeed a theft,
A crime of sacrilege against the past,
Which yet I had no courage to forgo—
From out the casket where I buried it
Upon my marriage-morn.   Helpless I thrust
The pale thing in my breast, and took it forth,
And kissed it . . . out among the trees I ran   .
The meadow-hay new-reaped . . . I saw him come;
He kissed me after thirty years . . .   I
        God
The younger Bertha caught her in her arms,
And dried her tears.

                    Well-pleased the King arose
To vindicate her fame; but Hilary cried,
" This was appealed to God, and He has judged:
There one adulterer lies; the other waits
The sentence of the King.   Who looks with lust
Commits adultery.   Be strong; do right.
Dare you annul God's manifest decree ?
Do you believe in God, Emanuel—
No shifting thought of man's, a living God ? '

A poignant voice from out his hollow casque;
Whereat the King delayed the judgment, dulled
By nerveless doubt.

           But Bertha laughed, ' Believe
In God!'—shaking her loosened mane of gold
From off her face, and with her heavy-lashed
And azure-watered eyelids clearing up
Her clouded vision—' I believe in God!
And He inspires me now to understand
His purpose in my lover's overthrow.
Doubtless He needed him in Heaven to be
His champion against some challenger,
Or to explore a new-made tract of worlds.
Me He requires to signify to men
That those obey Him best and do His will
Implicitly, who on themselves alone
Rely in peril of a tarnished name;
For power divine in plenitude enough
To conquer every ill endows us all,
If valiantly we give it scope to work
By taking on ourselves the total war.
Had Godfrey beaten Hilary, ' Oh ay '—
The gossips and the sponsors of report
Would certainly have made the accepted word—
' The hardy, brilliant lover overthrows
The age-bent husband ' Now myself can clear
From every foul aspersion Godfrey's fame.

Mine, and my children's.   Wherefore I demand
The Ordeal by Fire, Emanuel.'

' I grant it,' said the King, feeling himself
Heroic: ' I believe in God and you.
Choose, then: the bar; the ring?'

        But Hilary said,
' The way of ploughshares heated hot remains
The ordeal provided by the law.'

' The ploughshares!' said the King, held in the trap
Of code that men will set to catch themselves.
' None ever traverse them uncharred, and few
Escape with life.'

      ' But I uncharred shall pass,'
The victim said.   ' Sir, I appeal to God
Within me and about me and above
To bear me scathless through the fiercest test.
Heat hot your ploughshares—now!'

        Her children quailed:
' No, mother—no!' they whispered.   ' What!' she
   cried,
' You also doubt your mother's chastity
And God's omnipotence and rectitude!'
Abashed they fell behind her.

Still the King
Debated with himself: but from the crowd
A tigrish clamour burst, and watering mouths
Gnashed as they roared, 'The ploughshares! Heat
    them hot!'

'Hark!' said the King, 'it is the voice of God!
Prepare the ordeal chosen and ordained.'

So when the evening threw across the west
Fabrics of vapour fine as treasured lace—
Dishevelled, faded, stained with crimson, trailed
And dipped in sacramental chalices
Of sunset unforgotten while love lasts—
Upon the damasked meadow fires were built
Beside the sounding threshold of the sea:
Nine furnaces, fierce-tempered, wherewithal
The snoring bellows, plied by eager hands,
Imparted to the iron the sexual hate
Obscurely rankling in the heart of life,
And now unloosed against the innocent.
As at a fair men laughed obscenely, trolled
The vapid catches ballad-mongers hawked,
And munched the wares of wayside merchantmen.
Upon the City wall strange women climbed—
No nearer might they stand: men ruled it so—
To watch their sister's martyrdom, unawed,
Or with a dull disquietude, or to pray:

For even soulless women sometimes pray
As headless insects buzz.   Emanuel
Sat in a chair of state, and gripped the arms,
Teeth clenched, eyes fixed, extorting from his soul
Belief that God would do what he desired.
Sir Hilary stood by, the ripened grudge
Of twenty years triumphant in his eyes,
And in his rigid heart a holy sense
Of dreadful duty done—one drop of gall,
One only in his vengeful cup: the King
In every charitable name had driven
The children, guarded, out of sight and sound
Of Bertha's hazard: thus the simpletons,
Who liked their father little and adored
The adulteress, were not to see the end!

Blindfolded, in her shroud, with naked feet,
She waited for the signal to advance.

'Is all prepared ?' the King demanded.   Ay;
All was prepared.   Aghast and tremulous,
He turned to Bertha: 'Are you ready, now ?'

'Ready,' she said, clear-voiced, 'God helping me!'
'What is your plea ?' he asked; for this the law re-
      quired.

She answered: 'If in thought or deed

I once betrayed my husband's trust, may death
Lay hold of me and drag me shrieking down
A branded corpse among the smouldering blades.'

'In God's great heart the issue lies.   Proceed.'
This said, the King bent down his twitching face
In prayer; for even men of parts will pray
Against the wrong instead of smiting it,
Besotted with a creed.

                                        The farriers,
Aglow, begrimed and moist with smoky sweat,
Their ready pinchers on the coulters clasped
And plucked them forth, sprinkling the dewy green
With jets of dying embers.   Placed apart
At intervals irregular, the nine
Deep notes of carmine pulsed in unison
Upon the hissing turf.   Trumpet and drum
Announced the ordeal; then softly raised
A funeral dirge as Bertha, breathing quick,
Set out upon her march.   She placed her foot,
Her naked buoyant foot, dew-drenched and white,
She placed it firmly on the first red edge,
Leapt half her height, and with a hideous cry
Fell down face-foremost brained upon the next.
They took her from among the smouldering blades,
A branded corpse, and laid her on the bier
Prepared: alive or dead, the record told   K

Of none who trod this fiery path uncharred
The miserable King arose and turned
In haggard silence toward the city.

                                    ' Sir,'
Said Hilary in an icy voice, ' the law
Exacts your sentence.'

                    ' Bloody, hellish beast!'
Burst out Emanuel, weak and broken.

                                ' Sir,'
Said Hilary, ' you stand for God, and must
Pronounce the doom which he has dumbly wrought.
You know the form.'

                    Then sullenly the King:
' Bertha, the wife of Hilary, is proved
A foul adulteress upon her own appeal
To Heaven, and in the market-place forthwith
Shall be consumed by fire.'

                        ' So let it be,'
The multitude replied.   So was it done.
And while the harlots and the prodigals
Jested and danced about the blazing corpse,
The moon, dispensing delegated light,
Behind the City stealthily arose;

And, fresh with scent of meadow-hay new-reaped,
The land-breeze bore to many a mariner,
Outward or homeward bound, the sweetest news,
Across the sounding threshold of the sea.

ST GEORGE'S DAY

BASIL   MENZIES   PERCY   BRIAN   HERBERT   SANDY

Herbert : I hear the lark and linnet sing;
I hear the whitethroat's alto ring.

Menzies : I hear the idle workmen sigh;
I hear his hungry children cry.

Sandy : Still sad and brooding over ill:
Why listen to discordant tones?

Herbert : We dream, we sing, we drive the quill
To keep the flesh upon our bones.
Therefore what trade have we with wrongs,
With ways and woes that spoil our songs?

Menzies : None, none!   Alas, there lies the sting!
We see, we feel, but cannot aid;
We hide our foolish heads and sing :
We live, we die; and all is said.

Herbert : To wonder-worlds of old romance
Our aching thoughts for solace run.

Brian : And some have stolen fire from France.

Sandy : And some adore the Midnight sun.

Menzies : I, too, for light the world explore.
And trembling, tread where angels trod;
Devout at every shrine adore,
And follow after each new god.
But by the altar everywhere
I find the money-changer's stall;
And littering every temple-stair
The sick and sore like maggots crawl.

Basil : Your talk is vain; your voice is hoarse.

Menzies : I would they were as hoarse and vain
As their wide-weltering spring and source
Of helpless woe, of wrath insane.

Herbert : Why will you hug the coast of Hell?

Brian : Why antedate the Judgment Dav?

Menzies : Nay, flout me not; you know me well.

Basil : Right, comrade! Give your fancy way.

Menzies : I cannot see the stars and flowers,
Nor hear the lark's soprano ring,
Because a ruddy darkness lowers
For ever, and the tempests sing.
I see the strong coerce the weak,
And labour overwrought rebel;
I hear the useless treadmill creak,
The prisoner, cursing in his cell;
I see the loafer-burnished wall;
I hear the rotting match-girl whine;
I see the unslept switchman fall;
I hear the explosion in the mine;
I see along the heedless street
The sandwichmen trudge through the mire;
I hear the tired quick tripping feet
Of sad, gay girls who ply for hire.

Basil : To brood on feeble woe at length
Must drive the sanest thinker mad;
Consider rather weal and strength.

Menzies : On what foundations do they stand ?
I mark the sable ironclad
In every sea; in every land,
An army, idling on the chain
Of rusty peace that chafes and frets
Its seven-leagued limbs, and bristled mane
Of glittering baycnets;

The glowing blast, the fire-shot smoke
Where guns are forged and armour-plate;
The mammoth hammer's pounding stroke;
The din of our dread iron date.
And always divers undertones
Within the roaring tempest throb—
The chink of gold, the labourer's groans,
The infant's wail, the woman's sob.
Hoarsely they beg of Fate to give
A little lightening of their woe,
A little time to love, to live,
A little time to think and know.
I see where from the slums may rise
Some unexpected dreadful dawn—
The gleam of steeled and scowling eyes,
A flash of women's faces wan!

Basil: This is St George's Day.
Menzies: St George? A wretched thief I vow.

Herbert: Nay, Menzies, you should rather say,
St George for Merry England, now!

Sandy: That surely is a phantom cry,
Hollow and vain for many years.

Menzies: I hear the idle workmen sigh;
I hear the drip of women's tears.

Herbert: I hear the lofty lark,
The lowly nightingale.

Basil: The present is a dungeon dark
Of social problems.   Break the gaol!
Get out into the splendid Past
Or bid the splendid Future hail.

Menzies: Nor then, nor now, nor first, nor last,
I know.   The slave of ruthless Law,
To me Time seems a dungeon vast
Where Life lies rotting in the straw.

Basil: I care not for your images
Of Life and Law.   I want to sing
Of England and of Englishmen
Who made our country what it is.

Herbert: And I to praise the English Spring.

Percy: St George for Merry England, then!

Menzies: There is no England now, I fear.

Basil: No England, say you, and since when?

Menzies: Cockney and Celt and Scot are here,
And Democrats and ' ans ' and ' ists '

In clubs and cliques and divers lists;
But now we have no Englishmen.

Basil : You utter what you never felt,
I know.   By bog and mount and fen,
No Saxon, Norman, Scot, or Celt
I find, but only Englishmen.

Herbert : In all our hedges roses bud.

Basil : And thought and speech are more than blood.

Herbert : Away with spleen, and let us sing
The praises of the English Spring!

Basil : In weeds of gold and purple hues
Glad April bursts with piping news
Of swifts and swallows come again,
And of the tender pensive strain
The bulfinch sings from bush to bush.

Percy: And oh! the blackbird and the thrush
Interpret as no master may
The meaning of the night and day.

Sandy : They catch the whispers of the breeze
And weave them into melodies.

Brian : They utter for the hours that pass
The purpose of their moments bright.

Basil : They speak the passion of the grass,
That grows so stoutly day and night.

Herbert : St George for merry England then!
For we are all good Englishmen!

Percy : We stand as our forefathers stood
For Liberty's and Conscience' sake.

Herbert : We are the sons of Robin Hood,
The sons of Hereward the Wake.

Percy : The sons of yeomen, English-fed,
Ready to feast, or drink or fight.

Herbert · The sons of kings—of Hal and Ned,
Who kept their island right and tight.

Percy : The sons of Cromwell's Ironsides,
Who knew no king but God above.

Basil : We are the sons of English brides,
Who married Englishmen for love.

Sandy : Oh, now I see Fate's means and ends!
The Bruce and Wallace wight I ken,
Who saved old Scotland from its friends,
Were mighty northern Englishmen.

Brian : And Parnell, who so greatly fought
Against a wanton useless yoke,
With Fate inevitably wrought
That Irish should be English folk.

Basil : By bogland, highland, down, and fen,
All Englishmen, all Englishmen!

Menzies : There is no England now, I say—

Brian : No England now!   My grief, my grief !

Menzies : We lie widespread, the dragon-prey
Of any Cappadocian thief.
In Arctic and Pacific seas
We lounge and loaf: and either pole
We reach with sprawling colonies—
Unwieldy limbs that lack a soul.

Basil : St George for Greater England, then!
The Boreal and the Austral men!
They reverence the heroic roll

Of Englishmen who sang and fought:
They have a soul, a mighty soul,
The soul of English speech and thought.

Sandy : And when the soul of England slept—

Basil : St George for foolish England, then!—

Sandy : Lo!   Washington and Lincoln kept
America for Englishmen!

Basil : Hurrah!   The English people reigns
Across the wide Atlantic flood!
It could not bind itself in chains!
For Yankee blood is English blood.

Herbert : And here the spring is queen
In robes of white and green.

Percy : In chestnut sconces opening wide
Tapers shall burn some fresh May morn.

Brian : And the elder brightens the highway side,
And the briony binds the thorn.

Sandy : White is the snow of the leafless sloe
The saxifrage by the sedge,

And white the lady-smocks a-row
And sauce-alone in the hedge.

Basil: England is in her Spring;
She only begins to be.
Oh! for an organ voice to sing
The summer I can see!
But the Past is there; and a mole may know,
And a bat may understand,
That we are the people wherever we go—
Kings by sea and land!

Herbert: And the spring is crowned and stoled
In purple and in gold.

Percy: Wherever light, wherever shade is,
Gold and purple may be seen.

Brian: Gold and purple lords-and-ladies
Tread a measure on the green.

Herbert: In deserts where the wild wind blows
Blossoms the magic hæmony.

Percy: Deep in the Chiltern woodland glows
The purple pasque anemone.

Basil: And England still grows great
And never shall grow old;

Within our hands we hold
The world's fate.

Menzies : We hold the world's fate?
The cry seems out of date.

Basil : Not while a single Englishman
Can work with English brains and bones!
Awaiting us since time began,
The swamps of ice, the wastes of flame!
In Boreal and Austral zones
Took life and meaning when we came.
The Sphinx that watches by the Nile
Has seen great empires pass away·
The mightiest lasted but a while;
Yet ours shall not decay.
Because, although red blood may flow,
And ocean shake with shot,
Not England's sword but England's Word
Undoes the Gordian Knot.
Bold tongue, stout heart, strong hand, brave brow
The world's four quarters win;
And patiently with axe and plough
We bring the deserts in.

Menzies : Whence comes this patriotic craze?
Spare us at least the hackneyed brag
About the famous English flag.

Basil: I'll spare no flourish of its praise.
Where'er our flag floats in the wind
Order and justice dawn and shine.
The dusky myriads of Ind,
The swarthy tribes far south the line,
And all who fight with lawless law,
And all with lawless men who cope
Look hitherward across the brine,
For we are the world's forlorn hope.

Menzies: That makes my heart leap up!   Hurrah!
We are the world's forlorn hope!

Herbert: And with the merry birds we sing
The praises of the English Spring.

Percy: Iris and orchis now unfold.

Brian: The drooping-leaved laburnums ope
In thunder-showers of greenish gold.

Menzies: And we are the world's forlorn hope!

Sandy: The lilacs shake their dancing plumes
Of lavender, mauve, and heliotrope.

Herbert: The speedwell on the highway blooms.

Menzies : And we are the world's forlorn hope!

Sandy : Skeletons lurk in every street.

Herbert : We push and strike for air and scope.

Brian : The pulses of rebellion beat
Where want and hunger skulk and mope.

Menzies : But though we wander far astray
And oft in gloomy darkness grope,
Fearless we face the blackest day,
For we are the world's forlorn hope.

Sandy : St George for Merry England then!
For we are all good Englishmen!

Basil : St George for Greater England then!
The Boreal and the Austral men!

All : By bogland, highland, down, and fen,
All Englishmen, all Englishmen!
Who with their latest breath shall sing
Of England and the English Spring!

MIDSUMMER DAY

BASIL   SANDY   HERBERT

Sandy: I cannot write, I cannot think;
  'Tis half delight and half distress:
My memory stumbles on the brink
  Of some unfathomed happiness—

Of some old happiness divine.
  What haunting scent, what haunting note,
What word, or what melodious line,
  Sends my heart throbbing to my throat?

Basil: What? thrilled with happiness to-day,
  The longest day in all the year,
Which we must spend in making hay
  By threshing straw in Fleet Street here!

What scent? what sound?   The odour stale
  Of watered streets; the rumour loud
Of hoof and wheel on road and rail,
  The rush and trample of the crowd!

Herbert : Humming the song of many a lark,
  Out of the sea, across the shires,
The west wind blows about the park,
  And faintly stirs the Fleet Street wires.

Perhaps it sows the happy seed
  That blossoms in your memory;
Certain of many a western mead,
  And hill and stream it speaks to me.

Basil : Go on: of rustic visions tell
  Till I forget the wilderness
Of sooty brick, the dusty smell,
  The jangle of the printing-press.

Herbert : I hear the woodman's measured stroke;
  I see the amber streamlet glide—
Above, the green gold of the oak
  Fledges the gorge on either side.

A thatched roof shines athwart the gloom
  Of the high moorland's darksome ground;
Far off the surging rollers boom,
  And fill the shadowy wood with sound.

Basil : You have pronounced the magic sign!
  The city with its thousand years,
Like some embodied mood of mine
  Uncouth, prodigious, disappears.

I stand upon a lowly bridge,
   Moss-grown beside the old Essex home;
Over the distant purple ridge
   The clouds arise in sultry foam;

In many a cluster, wreath and chain
   A silvery vapour hangs on high,
And snowy scarfs of silken grain
   Bedeck the blue slopes of the sky;

The wandering water sighs and calls,
   And breaks into a chant that rings
Beneath the vaulted bridge, then falls
   And under heaven softly sings;

A light wind lingers here and there,
   And whispers in an unknown tongue
The passionate secrets of the air,
   That never may by man be sung:

Low, low, it whispers; stays, and goes;
   It comes again; again takes flight;
And like a subtle presence grows
   And almost gathers into sight.

Sandy : The wind that stirs the Fleet Street wires
   And roams and quests about the Park,
That wanders all across the shires,
   Humming the song of many a lark—

The wind—it is the wind, whose breath,
   Perfumed with roses, wakes in me
From shrouded slumbers deep as death
   A yet unfaded memory.

Basil: About Midsummer, every hour
   Ten thousand rosebuds opening blush,
The land is all one rosy bower,
   And rosy odours haunt and flush

The winds of heaven up and down:
   On the top-gallant of the air
The lark, the pressman in the town
   Breathe only rosy incense rare.

Sandy: And I, enchanted by the rose,
   Remember when I first began
To know what in its bosom glows
   Exhaling scent ambrosian.

A child, at home in streets and quays,
   The city tumult in my brain,
I only knew of tarnished trees,
   And skies corroding vapours stain.

One summer—Time upon my head
   Had showered the curls of years eleven—
Me, for a month, good fortune led
   Where trees are green and hills kiss heaven.

By glen and mountain, moor and lawn,
   Burn-side and sheep-path, day and night,
I wandered, a belated faun,
   All sense, all wonder, all delight.

And once at eve I climbed a hill,
   Burning to see the sun appear,
And watched the jewelled darkness fill
   With lamps and clustered tapers clear.

At last the strongest stars were spent;
   A glimmering shadow overcame
The swarthy-purple firmament,
   And throbbed and kindled into flame;

The pallid day, the trembling day
   Put on her saffron wedding-dress,
And watched her bridegroom far away
   Soar through the starry wilderness.

I clasped my hands and closed my eyes,
   And tears relieved my ecstasy:
I dared not watch the sun arise;
   Nor knew what magic daunted me:

And yet the roses seemed to tell
   More than the morn, had I but known
The meaning of the fragrant smell
   That bound me with a subtle zone.

But in the gloaming when we played
    At hide-and-seek, and I with her
Behind a rose-bush hid, afraid
    To meet her gaze, to breathe, or stir,

The dungeon of my sense was riven,
    The beauty of the world laid bare,
A great wind caught me up to heaven
    Upon a cloud of golden hair;

And mouth touched mouth; and love was born;
    And when our wondering vision blent,
We found the meaning of the morn,
    The meaning of the rose's scent.

Ah me! ah me! since then! since then!

Herbert : Nay, nay; let self-reproaches be!
Now that this thought is throned again,
    Be zealous for its sovereignty.

Basil: And brave, great Nature must be thanked,
    And we must worship on our knees,
And hold for ever sacro-sanct
    Such dewy memories as these.

ALL HALLOW'S EVE

BASIL   MENZIES   BRIAN   PERCY

Brian : Tearfully sinks the pallid sun.

Menzies : Bring in the lamps: Autumn is done.

Percy : Nay, twilight silvers the flashing drops;
 And a whiter fall is behind.

Brian : And the wild east mouths the chimney-tops,
 The Pandean pipes of the wind.

Menzies : The dripping ivy drapes the walls;
 The drenched red creepers flare;
And the draggled chestnut plumage falls
 In every park and square.

Percy : Nay, golden garlands strew the way
 For the old triumph of decay.

Basil : And I know, in a living land of spells—
 In an excellent land of rest,
Where a crimson fount of sunset wells
 Out of the darkling west—

That the poplar, the willow, the scented lime,
    Full-leaved in the shining air
Tarry as if the enchanter time
    Had fixed them deathless there.

In arbours and noble palaces
    A gallant people live
With every manner of happiness
    The amplest life can give.

Percy: Where? where? In Elfland?

        Menzies: No; oh no!
    In Elfland is no rest,
But rumour and stir and endless woe
    Of the unfulfilled behest—
The doleful yoke of the Elfin folk
    Since first the sun went west.

The cates they eat and the wine they drink,
    Savourless nothings are;
The hopes they cherish, the thoughts they think
    Are neither near nor far;
And well they know they cannot go
    Even to a desert star:

One planet is all their poor estate,
    Though a million systems roll;

They are dogged and worried, early and late,
    As the demons nag a soul,
By the moon and the sun, for they never can shun
    Time's tyrannous control.

The haughty delicate style they keep
    Only the blind can see;
On holynights in the forest deep,
    When they make high revelry
Under the moon, the dancing tune
    Is the wind in a cypress tree.

They burn the elfin midnight oil
    Over their tedious lore;
They spin the sand; and still they toil
    Though their inmost hearts are sore—
The doleful yoke of the restless folk
    For ever and ever more.

But could you capture the elfin queen
    Who once was Cæsar's prize,
Daunt and gyve her with glances keen
    Of unimpassioned eyes,
And hear unstirred her magic word,
    And scorn her tears and sighs,

Lean would she seem at once, and old;
    Her rosy mouth decayed;

Her heavy tresses of living gold,
  All withered in the braid;
In your very sight the dew and the light
  Of her eyes would parch and fade;

And she, the immortal phantom dame,
  Would vanish from your ken;
For the fate of the elves is nearly the same
  As the terrible fate of men:
To love; to rue: to be and pursue
  A flickering wisp of the fen.

We must play the game with a careless smile,
  Though there's nothing in the hand;
We must toil as if it were worth our while
  Spinning our ropes of sand;
And laugh and cry, and live and die
  At the waft of an unseen wand.

But the elves, besides the endless woe
  Of the unfulfilled behest,
Have only a phantom life, and so
  They neither can die nor rest—
Have no real being at all, and know
  That therefore they never can rest—
The doleful yoke of the deathless folk
  Since first the sun went west.

Percy: Then where is the wonderful land of spells,
Where a crimson fount of sunset wells,
And the poplar, the willow, the scented lime
Tarry, full-leaved, till the winter-time,
Where endless happiness life can give,
And only heroic people live ?

Basil: We know, we know, we spinners of sand!
In the heart of the world is that gracious land;
And it never can fade while the sap returns,
While the sun gives light, and the red blood burn.

EPILOGUE TO FLEET STREET ECLOGUES

ARTIST   VOTARY

Votary: What gloomy outland region have I won?

Artist: This is the Vale of Hinnom. What are you?

Votary: A Votary of Life.   I thought this tract,
With rubbish choked, had been a thoroughfare
For many a decade now.

        Artist: No highway here!
And those who enter never can return.

Votary: But since my coming is an accident—

Artist: All who inhabit Hinnom enter there
By accident, carelessly cast aside,
Or self-inducted in an evil hour.

Votary: But I shall walk about it and go forth.

Artist: I said so when I came; but I am here.

Votary : What brought you hither ?

          Artist : Chance, no other power:
My tragedy is common to my kind.—
Once from a mountain-top at dawn I saw
My life pass by, a pageant of the age,
Enchanting many minds with sound and light,
Array and colour, deed, device and spell.
And to myself I said aloud, ‘ When thought
And passion shall be rooted deep, and fleshed
In all experience man may dare, yet front
His own interrogation unabashed:
Winged also, and inspired to cleave with might
Abysses and the loftiest firmament:
When my capacity and art are ranked
Among the powers of nature, and the world
Awaits my message, I will paint a scene
Of life and death, so tender, so humane,
That lust and avarice lulled awhile, shall gaze
With open countenances; broken hearts,
The haunt, the shrine, and wailing-place of woe,
Be comforted with respite unforeseen,
And immortality reprieve despair.’
The vision beckoned me; the prophecy,
That smokes and thunders in the blood of youth,
Compelled unending effort, treacherous
Decoys of doom although these tokens were.
Across the wisdom and the wasted love

Of some who barred the way my pageant stepped:
'Thus are all triumphs paved,' I said; but soon,
Entangled in the tumult of the times,
Sundered and wrecked, it ceased to pace my thought,
Wherein alone its airy nature strode;
While the smooth world, whose lord I deemed myself,
Unsheathed its claws and blindly struck me down,
Mangled my soul for sport, and cast me out
Alive in Hinnom where human offal rots,
And fires are heaped against the tainted air.

Votary: Escape!

   Artist: I tried, as you will try; and then,
Dauntless, I cried, 'At midnight, darkly lit
By drifts of flame whose ruddy varnish dyes
The skulls and rounded knuckles light selects
Flickering upon the refuse of despair,
Here, as it should the costly pageant ends;
And here with my last strength, since I am I,
Here will I paint my scene of life and death:
Not that I dreamt of when the eager dawn,
And inexperience, stubborn parasite
Of youth and manhood, flattered in myself
And in a well-pleased following, vanities
Of hope, belief, good-will, the embroidered stuff
That masks the cruel eyes of destiny;
But a new scene profound and terrible

As Truth, the implacable antagonist.
And yet most tender, burning, bitter-sweet
As are the briny tears and crimson drops
Of human anguish, inconsolable
Throughout all time, and wept in every age
By open wounds and cureless, such as I,
Whence issues nakedly the heart of life.'

Votary: What canvas and what colour could you find
To paint in Hinnom so intense a scene ?

Artist: I found and laid no colour.   Look about!
On the flame-roughened darkness whet your eyes.
This needs no deeper hue; this is the thing:
Millions of people huddled out of sight,
The offal of the world.

                    Votary : I see them now,
In groups, in multitudes, in hordes, and some
Companionless, ill-lit by tarnished fire
Under the towering darkness ceiled with smoke;
Erect, supine, kneeling or prone, but all
Sick-hearted and aghast among the bones.

Artist: Here pine the subtle souls that had no root.
No home below, until disease or shame
Undid the once-so-certain destiny
Imagined for the Brocken-sprite of self,

While earth, which seemed a pleasant inn of dreams,
Unveiled a tedious death-bed and a grave.

Votary : I see!   The dissillusioned geniuses
Who fain would make the world sit up, by Heaven!
And dig God in the ribs, and who refuse
Their own experience: would-bes, theorists,
Artistic natures, failed reformers, knaves
And fools incompetent or overbold,
Broken evangelists and debauchees,
Inebriates, criminals, cowards, virtual slaves.

Artist : The world is old; and countless strains of
        blood
Are now effete: these loathsome ruined lives
Are innocent—if life itself be good.
Inebriate, coward, artist, criminal—
The nicknames unintelligence expels
Remorse with when the conscience hints that all
Are guilty of the misery of one.
Look at these women: broken chalices,
Whose true aroma of the spring is spilt
In thankless streets and with the sewage blent.

Votary : Harlots, you mean; the scavengers of love,
Who sweep lust from our thresholds—needful brooms
In every age; the very bolts indeed
That clench and rivet solidarity.

All this is as it has been and shall be:
I see it, note it, and go hence.   Farewell.

Artist : Here I await you.

          *   *   *   *

               Votary : There is no way out.

Artist : But we are many.   What?   So pinched
      and pale
At once!   Weep, and take courage.   This is best,
Because the alternative is not to be.

Votary : But I am nothing yet, have made no mark
Upon my time; and, worse than nothing now,
Must wither in a nauseous heap of tares.
Why am I outcast who so loved the world?
How did I reach this place?   Hush!   Let me think.
I said—what did I say and do?   Nothing to mourn.
I trusted life, and life has led me here.

Artist : Where dull endurance only can avail.
Scarcely a tithe of men escape this fate;
And not a tithe of those who suffer know
Their utter misery.

               Votary : And must this be
Now and for ever, and has it always been?

M

Artist : Worse now than ever and ever growing worse.
Men as they multiply use up mankind
In greater masses and in subtler ways:
Ever more opportunity, more power
For intellect, the proper minister
Of life, that will usurp authority,
With lightning at its beck and prisoned clouds.
I mean that electricity and steam
Have set a barbarous fence about the earth,
And made the oceans and the continents
Preserved estates of crafty gather-alls;
Have loaded labour with a shotted chain,
And raised the primal curse a thousand powers.

Votary: What!   Are there honest labourers outcast
        here ?
Dreamers, pococurantes, wanton bloods
In plenty and to spare; but surely work
Attains another goal than Hinnom!

                              Artist : Look!
Seared by the sun and carved by cold or blanched
In darkness; gnarled and twisted all awry
By rotting fogs; lamed, limb-lopped, cankered, burst,
The outworn workers!

                    Votary : I take courage then!
Since workers here abound it must be right
That men should end in Hinnom.

Artist : Right!   How right ?
The fable of the world till now records
Only the waste of life: the conquerors,
Tyrants and oligarchs, and men of ease,
Among the myriad nations, peoples, tribes,
Need not be thought of: earth's inhabitants,
Man, ape, dinornis for a moment breathe,
In misery die, and to oblivion
Are dedicated all.   Consider still
The circumstance that most appeals to men:
Eternal siege and ravage of the source
Of being, of beauty, and of all delight,
The hell of whoredom.   God!   The hourly waste
Of women in the world since time began!

Votary : I think of it.

Artist : And of the waste of men
In war—pitiful soldiers, battle-harlots.

Votary : That also I consider.

Artist : Weaklings, fools
In millions who must end disastrously;
The willing hands and hearts, in millions too,
Paid with perdition for a life of toil;
The blood of women, a constant sacrifice,
Staining the streets and every altar-step;
The blood of men poured out in endless wars;

No hope, no help; the task, the stripes, the woe
Augmenting with the ages.   Right, you say!

Votary : Do you remember how the moon appears
Illumining the night?

          Artist : What has the moon
To do with Hinnom ?

          Votary: Call the moon to mind.
Can you ?   Or have you quite forgotten all
The magic of her beams ?

          Artist : Oh no!   The moon
Is the last memory of ample thought,
Of joy and loveliness that one forgets
In this abode.   Since first the tide of life
Began to ebb and flow in human veins,
The targe of lovers' looks, their brimming fount
Of dreams and chalice of their sighs; with peace
And deathless legend clad and crowned, the moon!

Votary : But I adore it with a newer love,
Because it is the offal of the globe.
When from the central nebula our orb,
Outflung, set forth upon its way through space,
Still towards its origin compelled to lean
And grope in molten tides, a belt of fire,
Home-sick, burst off at last, and towards the sun

Whirling, far short of its ambition fell,
Insphered a little distance from the earth
There to bethink itself and wax and wane,
The moon!

Artist: I see! I know! You mean that you
And I, and foiled ambitions every one
In every age; the outworn labourers,
Pearls of the sewer, idlers, armies, scroyles,
The offal of the world, will somehow be—
Are now a lamp by night, although we deem
Ourselves disgraced, forlorn; even as the moon,
The scum and slag of earth, that, if it feels,
Feels only sterile pain, gladdens the mountains
And the spacious sea.

Votary: I mean it.   And I mean
That the deep thoughts of immortality
And of our alienage, inventing gods
And paradise and wonders manifold,
Are rooted in the centre.   We are fire,
Cut off and cooled a while: and shall return,
The earth and all thereon that live and die,
To be again candescent in the sun,
Or in the sun's intenser, purer source.
What matters Hinnom for an hour or two ?
Arise and let us sing; and, singing, build
A tabernacle even with these ghastly bones.

IN ROMNEY MARSH

As I went down to Dymchurch Wall,
 I heard the South sing o'er the land;
I saw the yellow sunlight fall
 On knolls where Norman churches stand.

And ringing shrilly, taut and lithe,
 Within the wind a core of sound,
The wire from Romney town to Hythe
 Alone its airy journey wound.

A veil of purple vapour flowed
 And trailed its fringe along the Straits;
The upper air like sapphire glowed;
 And roses filled Heaven's central gates.

Masts in the offing wagged their tops;
 The swinging waves pealed on the shore;
The saffron beach, all diamond drops
 And beads of surge, prolonged the roar.

As I came up from Dymchurch Wall,
  I saw above the Downs' low crest
The crimson brands of sunset fall,
  Flicker and fade from out the west.

Night sank: like flakes of silver fire
  The stars in one great shower came down;
Shrill blew the wind; and shrill the wire
  Rang out from Hythe to Romney town.

The darkly shining salt sea drops
  Streamed as the waves clashed on the shore;
The beach, with all its organ stops
  Pealing again, prolonged the roar.

A CINQUE PORT

BELOW the down the stranded town,
  What may betide forlornly waits,
With memories of smoky skies,
  When Gallic navies crossed the straits;
When waves with fire and blood grew bright,
And cannon thundered through the night.

With swinging stride the rhythmic tide
  Bore to the harbour barque and sloop;
Across the bar the ship of war,
  In castled stern and lanterned poop,
Came up with conquests on her lee,
The stately mistress of the sea.

Where argosies have wooed the breeze,
  The simple sheep are feeding now;
And near and far across the bar
  The ploughman whistles at the plough;
Where once the long waves washed the shore,
Larks from their lowly lodgings soar.

Below the down the stranded town
    Hears far away the rollers beat;
About the wall the seabirds call;
    The salt wind murmurs through the street;
Forlorn the sea's forsaken bride,
Awaits the end that shall betide.

LONDON

ATHWART the sky a lowly sigh
    From west to east the sweet wind carried;
The sun stood still on Primrose Hill;
    His light in all the city tarried:
The clouds on viewless columns bloomed
Like smouldering lilies unconsumed.

' Oh sweetheart, see! how shadowy,
    Of some occult magician's rearing,
Or swung in space of heaven's grace
    Dissolving, dimly reappearing,
Afloat upon ethereal tides
St. Paul's above the city rides!'

A rumour broke through the thin smoke
    Enwreathing abbey, tower, and palace,
The parks, the squares, the thoroughfares,
    The million-peopled lanes and alleys,
An ever-muttering prisoned storm,
The heart of London beating warm.

WAITING

Within unfriendly walls
  We starve—or starve by stealth.
Oxen fatten in their stalls;
  You guard the harrier's health:
They never can be criminals,
  And can't compete for wealth.
    From the mansion and the palace
      Is there any help or hail
    For the tenants of the alleys,
      Of the workhouse and the jail?

Though lands await our toil,
  And earth half-empty rolls,
Cumberers of English soil,
  We cringe for orts and doles—
Prosperity's accustomed foil,
  Millions of useless souls.
    In the gutters and the ditches
      Human vermin festering lurk—
  We, the rust upon your riches;
    We, the flaw in all your work.

Come down from where you sit;
  We look to you for aid.
Take us from the miry pit,
  And lead us undismayed:
Say, 'Even you, outcast, unfit,
    Forward with sword and spade!'
      And myriads of us idle
        Would thank you through our tears,
      Though you drove us with a bridle,
        And a whip about our ears!

From cloudy cape to cape
  The teeming waters seethe;
Golden grain and purple grape
  The regions overwreathe.
Will no one help us to escape?
  We scarce have room to breathe.
    You might try to understand us:
      We are waiting night and day
    For a captain to command us,
      And the word we must obey.

EARTH TO EARTH

WHERE the region grows without a lord,
  Between the thickets emerald-stoled,
In the woodland bottom the virgin sward,
    The cream of the earth, through depths of mold
      O'erflowing wells from secret cells,
While the moon and the sun keep watch and ward,
  And the ancient world is never old.

Here, alone, by the grass-green hearth
  Tarry a little: the mood will come!
Feel your body a part of earth;
    Rest and quicken your thought at home;
      Take your ease with the brooding trees;
Join in their deep-down silent mirth
  The crumbling rock and the fertile loam.

Listen and watch! The wind will sing;
  And the day go out by the western gate;
The night come up on her darkling wing;
    And the stars with flaming torches wait.
      Listen and see! And love and be
The day and the night and the world-wide thing
  Of strength and hope you contemplate.

No lofty Patron of Nature!   No;
  Nor a callous devotee of Art!
But the friend and the mate of the high and the low,
  And the pal to take the vermin's part,
    Your inmost thought divinely wrought,
In the grey earth of your brain aglow
  With the red earth burning in your heart.

PIPER, PLAY!

Now the furnaces are out,
  And the aching anvils sleep;
Down the road the grimy rout
  Tramples homeward twenty deep.
    Piper, play! Piper, play!
      Though we be o'erlaboured men,
      Ripe for rest, pipe your best!
      Let us foot it once again!

Bridled looms delay their din;
  All the humming wheels are spent;
Busy spindles cease to spin;
  Warp and woof must rest content.
    Piper, play! Piper, play!
      For a little we are free!
      Foot it girls and shake your curls,
        Haggard creatures though we be!

Racked and soiled the faded air
  Freshens in our holiday;
Clouds and tides our respite share;
  Breezes linger by the way.

Piper, rest!   Piper, rest!
   Now, a carol of the moon!
Piper, piper, play your best!
   Melt the sun into your tune!

We are of the humblest grade;
   Yet we dare to dance our fill:
Male and female were we made—
   Fathers, mothers, lovers still!
     Piper—softly; soft and low;
      Pipe of love in mellow notes,
     Till the tears begin to flow,
      And our hearts are in our throats.

Nameless as the stars of night
   Far in galaxies unfurled,
Yet we wield unrivalled might,
   Joints and hinges of the world!
     Night and day! night and day!
      Sound the song the hours rehearse!
     Work and play! work and play!
      The order of the universe!

Now the furnaces are out,
   And the aching anvils sleep;
Down the road a merry rout
   Dances homeward, twenty deep.

Piper, play! Piper, play!
   Wearied people though we be,
Ripe for rest, pipe your best!
   For a little we are free!

THE MAN FORBID

MANKIND has cast me out.   When I became
So close a comrade of the day and night,
Of earth and of the seasons of the year,
And so submissive in my love of life
And study of the world that I unknew
The past and names renowned, religion, art,
Inventions, thoughts, and deeds, as men unknow
What good and evil fate befell their souls
Before their bodies gave them residence,
(How the old letter haunts the spirit still!
As if the soul were other than the sum
The body's powers make up—a golden coin,
Amount of so much silver, so much bronze!)
I said, rejoicing, ' Now I stand erect,
' And am that which I am.'   Compassionate
I watched a motley crowd beside me bent
Beneath unsteady burdens, toppling loads
Of volumes, news and lore antique, that showered
About their ears to be re-edified
On aching heads and shoulders overtasked.
Yet were these hodmen cheerful, ignorant
Of woe whose character it is to seem

Predestined and an honourable care:
They read their books, re-read, and read again;
They balanced libraries upon their polls,
And tottered through the valley almost prone,
But certain they were nobler than the beasts.
I saw besides in fields and cities hordes
Of haggard people soaked in filth and slime
Wherewith they fed the jaded earth the while
Their souls of ordure stank; automata
That served machines whose tyrannous revolt
Enthralled their lords, as if the mistletoe
Displaying mournful gold and wintry pearls
On sufferance, should enchant the forest oak
To be its accident and parasite;
Wretches and monsters that were capable
Of joy and sorrow once, their bodies numbed,
Their souls deflowered, their reason disendowed
By noisome trades, or at the furnaces,
In drains and quarries and the sunless mines;
And myriads upon myriads, human still
Without redemption drudging till they died.

Aware how multitudes of those enslaved
No respite sought, but squandered leisure hours
Among the crowd whose choice or task it was
To balance libraries upon their polls,
I laughed a long low laugh with weeping strung,
A rosary of tears, to see mankind

So dauntless and so dull, and cried at last,
' Good people, honest people, cast them off
' And stand erect, for few are helped by books.
' What! will you die crushed under libraries ?
' Lo! thirty centuries of literature
' Have curved your spines and overborne your brains!
' Off with it—all of it!   Stand up; behold
' The earth; life, death, and day and night!
' Think not the things that have been said of these;
' But watch them and be excellent, for men
' Are what they contemplate.'

                    They mocked me: ' Yah!
' The fox who lost his tail!   Though you are crazed
' We have our wits about us.'
                              ' Nay,' I cried;
' There was besides an ape who lost his tail
' That he might change to man.   Undo the past!
' The rainbow reaches Asgard now no more;
' Olympus stands untenanted; the dead
' Have their serene abode in earth itself,
' Our womb, our nurture, and our sepulchre.
' Expel the sweet imaginings, profound
' Humanities and golden legends, forms
' Heroic, beauties, tripping shades, embalmed
' Through hallowed ages in the fragrant hearts
' And generous blood of men; the climbing thoughts
' Whose roots ethereal grope among the stars,

' Whose passion-flowers perfume eternity,
' Weed out and tear, scatter and tread them down;
' Dismantle and dilapidate high heaven.
' It has been said: Ye must be born again.
' I say to you: Men must be that they are.
' Philosophy, the juggling dupe who finds
' Astounding meanings in the Universe,
' Commodiously secreted by himself;
' Religion, that appoints the soul a flight
' Empyreal—hoods its vision then and plucks
' Its plumes, its arching pinions tethers down
' To flap about a laystall; Art sublime,
' The ancient harlot of the ages, she
' Whose wig of golden tinct, enamelled face
' And cushioned bosom rivet glowing looks,
' Whose scented flatulence diviner seems
' Than dulcet breath of girls who keep their trysts
' In hawthorn brakes devoutly, when the sap
' Bestirs the troubled forest and the winds
' Solace the moonlit earth with whispered news:
' Religion, Art, Philosophy—this God,
' This Beauty, this Idea men have filled
' The world with, study still, and still adore,
' Are only segments of the spirit's tail
' We must outgrow, if spirit would ascend,
' (Let Spirit be the word for body-and-soul!
' Will language ne'er be fused and forged anew ?)
' And quit the withering life of fear and shame,

' Of agony and pitiful desire
' To reign untailed in heaven hereafter—Laugh!
' The changing image seizes you.   Or thus:
' This Beauty, this Divinity, this Thought,
' This hallowed bower and harvest of delight
' Whose roots ethereal seemed to clutch the stars,
' Whose amaranths perfumed eternity,
' Is fixed in earthly soil enriched with bones
' Of used-up workers; fattened with the blood
' Of prostitutes, the prime manure; and dressed
' With brains of madmen and the broken hearts
' Of children.   Understand it, you at least
' Who toil all day and writhe and groan all night
' With roots of luxury, a cancer struck
' In every muscle: out of you it is
' Cathedrals rise and Heaven blossoms fair;
' You are the hidden putrefying source
' Of beauty and delight, of leisured hours,
' Of passionate loves and high imaginings;
' You are the dung that keeps the roses sweet.
' I say, uproot it; plough the land; and let
' A summer-fallow sweeten all the World.'

With mud bespattered, bruised with staves and stoned—
' You called us dung!'—me from their midst they
        drove.
Alone I went in darkness and in light,
Colour and sound attending on my steps,

And life and death, the ministers of men,
My constant company.   But in my heart
Of hearts I longed for human neighbourhood,
And bent my pride to win men back again.
I came, a penitent; and on my knees
I climbed their stairs; I thundered at their doors,
And cried, ' I am your brother; in your wrath,
' As brethren should, destroy me; at your hands
' I must have life or death: I cannot bear
' The outcast's fate.'

                              They bade me then proclaim
How seemed the World now in my penitence.
But when I rose to speak, their palaces,
Their brothels, slums, cathedrals, theatres,
Asylums, factories, exchanges, banks,
The patched-up world of heirlooms, hand-me-downs
That worm and moth dispute, of make-believe,
Of shoddy, pinchbeck, sweepings of the street,
Of war disguised, of unconcealed chicane,
Of shrivelled drudge and swollen parvenu,
Turned at my glance into that murky vale
Where patient hodmen on their rounded backs
Sustained the thought of thirty centuries,
Where multitudes of slaves renounced their rest
To balance libraries upon their polls;
Or to that giant oaf (for vision shifts
The world about like winds that shape the clouds)

Whose spiritual tail, most awkward now
That breeches hide the rump, is cherished still
With ursine piety; or to that bower
Of Heaven's Delight whose barbed and cancerous
    roots
Are struck in earthly soil enriched with blood
Of men and women.   As I saw I said:
(How could I else!) and bade them as before
' Arise!   Uproot the pleasance; plough the land,
' And let the World lie fallow.   Only then
' Can any seed of change have room to grow.'

They yelled upon me and their missiles flew;
But one arose to represent the World,
And at his nod their clamour ceased.   He said:
' There is no harbour here for such as you.
' You know not what you say nor understand
' How you have hurt yourself.   You cannot—fool,
' And answered as befits!—contrive to make
' A monkey human by caudatomy;
' Nor can humanity transcend itself
' By shearing off its spirit at the root.
' That of the tail is false analogy.
' Man springs from out the past: his tap-roots pierce
' The strata of the ages, drawing strength
' From every generation, every cult.
' The scission of the smallest rootlet harms
' His growth.'

Then turning he adjured the crowd:
‘ Be warned or be accursed!   This monster steps
‘ Beyond the scope and furthest bound of man:
‘ Mere mirror is his brain; his heart, mere husk.
‘ A waft of death comes from him.   Would you live
‘ Indifferent to your own delight, unmoved
‘ By kindred sorrow, and oblivious
‘ Of all your fath:rs did, then give him ear,
‘ And quit forever the resourceful past.
‘ I   know   you   will   not.   What!   Some   pause   to
        think ?
‘ Resort now to the knife and you will find
‘ ’Tis not an unbecoming, useless tail
‘ You sever manfully to be yourselves,
‘ But suicide of sou! that you commit.’

To me: ‘ You ask for life or death from us,
‘ Because you cannot bear the outcast’s fate.
‘ We disregard your claim: what you can bear
‘ Is no concern of ours: we cast you out.
‘ Your well-earned portion of the Universe
‘ Is isolation and eternal death.
‘ Cut off, an alien, here you have no home:
‘ No face shall ever gladden at your step,
‘ No woman long to see you.   Get you hence,
‘ And seek the desert; or since your soul is dead,
‘ Return your body to the earth at once,
‘ And let resolved oblivior triumph now.’

Gladly the World approved with hand and voice;
And one, a woman, offered me a knife:
‘And let resolved oblivion triumph now,’
She echoed.   Had it been my will to die,
I should not then have made the sacrifice
At the World’s bidding; but I chose to live,
For while I live the victory is mine.

So I went forth for evermore forbid
The company of men.   The Universe,
Systems and suns and all that breathes and is,
Appeared at first in that dread solitude
Only the momentary, insolent
Irruption of a glittering fantasy
Into the silent, empty Infinite.
But eyes and ears were given to me again:
With these a man may do; with these, endure.

I haunt the hills that overlook the sea.
Here in the Winter like a meshwork shroud
The sifted snow reveals the perished land,
And powders wisps of knotgrass dank and dead
That trail like faded locks on mouldering skulls
Unearthed from shallow burial.   With the Spring
The west-wind thunders through the budding hedge
That stems the furrowed steep—a sound of drums,
Of gongs and muted cymbals; yellow breasts
And brown wings whirl in gusts, fly chaffering, drop,

And surge in gusts again; in wooded coombs
The hyacinth with purple diapers
The russet beechmast, and the cowslips hoard
Their virgin gold in lucent chalices;
The sombre furze, all suddenly attired
In rich brocade, the enterprise in chief
And pageant of the season, overrides
The rolling land and girds the bosomed plain
That strips her green robe to a saffron shore
And steps into the surf where threads and scales
And arabesques of blue and emerald wave
Begin to damascene the iron sea;
While faint from upland fold and covert peal
The sheep-bell and the cuckoo's mellow chime.
Then when the sovereign light from which we came,
Of earth enamoured, bends most questioning looks,
I watch the land grow beautiful, a bride
Transfigured with desire of her great lord.
Betrothal-music of the tireless larks,
Heaven-high, heaven-wide possesses all the air,
And wreathes the shining lattice of the light
With chaplets, purple clusters, vintages
Of sound from the first fragrant breath and first
Tear-sprinkled blush of Summer to the deep
Transmuted fire, the smouldering golden moons,
The wine-stained dusk of Autumn harvest-ripe;
And I behold the period of Time,
When Memory shall devolve and Knowledge lapse

Wanting a subject, and the willing earth
Leap to the bosom of the sun to be
Pure flame once more in a new time begun:
Here, as I pace the pallid doleful hills
And serpentine declivities that creep
Unhonoured to the ocean's shifting verge,
Or where with prouder curve and greener sward,
Surmounting peacefully the restless tides,
The cliffed escarpment ends in stormclad strength.

-,
RNIA,

Lightning Source UK Ltd.
Milton Keynes UK
UKOW06f1855061015

259993UK00017B/716/P

9 781331 036951